It Only Hurts When I Polka

It Only Hurts When I Polka

Even More Tongue in Cheek Looks at Queer Life

Kevin Isom

Writers Club Press
San Jose New York Lincoln Shanghai

It Only Hurts When I Polka
Even More Tongue in Cheek Looks at Queer Life

Writers Club Press
an imprint of iUniverse.com, Inc.

For information address:
iUniverse.com, Inc.
5220 S 16th, Ste. 200
Lincoln, NE 68512
www.iuniverse.com

ISBN: 0-595-18370-0

Printed in the United States of America

With many thanks to the dedicated readers of my columns over the years, for their encouragement in putting my tongue in cheek for a second book.

CONTENTS

Other Books by Kevin Isom

Tongue in Cheek and Other Places: A Seriously Humorous Look at
Queer Life

ACKNOWLEDGEMENTS

Cover photo by Steven Eads Photography (www.steveneads.com). Cover model: Matt Fleck.

Thanks to Derek Scheidt and Keith Easterling for their editing skill.

Thanks to Clint Horne for his contributions of talent and time to *Will & Grace Under Pressure*, *Party of Five*, and others, and for providing inspiration to the author for four and a half years.

Start the Music.
Maestro, Grab Your Baton

Ask Me to Dance

Dancing is a lot like sex. Somebody leads, somebody follows, and the roles can be switched back and forth. There are good leads, and there are good follows. Sometimes toes get pinched. And if it's a great dance experience, there's an incredible rush when you really get going.

As I pondered putting together a second collection of columns, I realized that dance could offer some great metaphors for aspects of gay and lesbian life. Or at least give some good chapter headings. Good head is so hard to find, after all.

I tend to mine my life and relationships for material to write about. Some people find the pick axe a little uncomfortable at first, but they understand it's the price of knowing me. I also mine my interests, and of late, couples dancing has two-stepped to the top of my list.

So read on, and maybe you'll find that you, too, are a dancin' queen.

Dancin' Queen.
Getting into the Gay Groove

SHALL WE DANCE?

There's no doubt about it. When it comes to dancing—the kind one does at parties, in nightclubs, and in discos—gay men are infinitely better than their straight counterparts. It's as if all the good groove went into just ten percent of the population. (Deal with it, straight guys. We get a kick out of watching you lumber around on the occasional nights that we're dragged into breeder bars with our straight girlfriends. No need to send in the clowns!)

Even so, one of the most interesting phenomena of the past few years has been the growth, especially in the South, but elsewhere too, of a queer interest in country-western dancing. Shades of *Urban Cowboy*!

You walk into any of these clubs, and you see—once you learn how to look around the cowboy hats—a dance floor filled with male and female couples gliding and twirling around the dance floor as they two-step or waltz. Of course, those of us who are new to the gig sort of crawl around the dance floor. I once danced with a really good dancer who said, "Don't look at your feet. Just count." So I did. "Quick, quick, slow, slow, quick, quick, slow, slow—" Suddenly he gritted his teeth and growled, "IN YOUR HEAD!" I nicknamed him the "Dance Nazi."

Couples dancing of the two-stepping and waltzing sort turns out to be a lot of fun. It's a very different kind of satisfaction from the bump and groove disco scene. You're in each other's arms. You're as close or as far apart as you want to be—or safely can be without tripping, anyway. Someone leads, someone follows. Folks who can go either way are know as "versatile." Or "bi." And they tend to be able to get more dance partners.

Despite the greater possibilities of going both ways, I decided to learn to follow because (a) I have better things to do than figure out where we're heading on a crowded dance floor, and (b) it's a challenge for me to let someone else take control. I admit I back-lead like you wouldn't believe, but a good lead can just whip that control right away. Sort of a contest of wills. And thighs.

The upside of country-western dancing is that it's coupled, romantic, and fun. With a good partner, it's like flying around the dance floor together.

The downside is the country music. Actually, though I hate to admit it, country music's not so bad. A lot of it is really melodic. And some of the newer country singers have done a lot to glamorize the genre. Look at Shania Twain, the country-pop crossover star. She wears all those slinky outfits, and she's liked by straight men and gay men alike. The straight men like her because they want to get her out of those slinky outfits. The gay men just want to borrow them. Besides, most of the country dance clubs play some alternative music as well. Like Madonna.

But even as I've enjoyed the country-western dance thing, I've begun to wonder why we don't have queer clubs for any of the other couples dances out there? Like swing. Or Latin dancing. Or even the Viennese waltz. Wouldn't those dances be just as much fun?

I had a chance to test my theory recently when a good friend asked me to accompany him to his boss' daughter's wedding. My friend's boss, in an excess of "I'm okay, you're okay" had insisted that my friend bring a date to the wedding. When straight people do the right thing, you really can't disappoint them. So I agreed to go, figuring I'd make a decent corporate spouse stand-in, so long as I could manage to restrain my usual comments on bridesmaid fashions.

Since we had no intention of stumbling around a dance floor in front of hundreds of straight folks looking at the only two men waltzing together, we began practicing weeks before the wedding. We'd roll up the rugs in my friend's living room, push back the furniture to the walls, and hit the hardwoods as the stereo cranked out waltzes.

We agreed (I insisted) to practice the Viennese waltz, because I loved the twirling round and round the dance floor. Hey, I'm entitled to an Audrey Hepburn moment every now and then. My friend turned out to be a powerful lead, so I relaxed and followed as we became slowly better, punctuating our waltzing with turns and double turns (and the occasional dreaded triple lutz). When the wedding day came, we acquitted ourselves with the gayest of dignity.

After all this waltzing and two-stepping, now I can't wait to try the other couples dances out there.

Tango, anyone?

KISSING IN THE CHURCH OF JUDY-ISM

"'So there's Bill,' Hillary tells me, 'with a bunch of roses for me. That means my legs will be in the air all weekend long.' 'What,' I answered, 'you don't have a vase?'"

The audience roared, and comedienne Judy Tenuta, the aging but beautiful love goddess who should have gotten a sitcom long before Geena Davis, stroked her accordion. I was at a suburban comedy club to see her perform, along with my date, and my partnered friends, Keith and Doug.

Years before, I had come to see Judy perform at the same club, but then it was on a gay night at the comedy club. Tonight was just like any other night. I only spotted two or three tables of gay men scattered throughout the audience. We shared our long table with a group of pretty, fun young straight women, but the rest of the club seemed filled with true suburbanites. Some of them were of the poodle perm, out-lying county, family-tree-goes-straight-up variety. I almost wondered if we should be scared.

Judy quickly got the crowd rolling with her jokes, much of them gay friendly if not downright queer, and I began to forget who we were surrounded by. We were sharing a laugh, which, in my tongue in cheek view, transcends sexual orientation.

But that was all about to change.

Near the end of the show, Judy began her marriage in the church of Judy-ism shtick, and she asked the crowd if there were any married couples in the audience. My friends Keith and Doug have been together for seven years, so Doug's hand shot straight up in the air, with Keith's not far behind.

Since we were seated down front, Judy immediately asked them where their wives were. They pointed at each other, and Judy screamed delightedly. She summarily ordered Keith and Doug on stage, to cheers from our table, laughter from others, and horrified stares from yet others.

Judy then demanded, "Okay, who's the bottom?" The straight folks in the audience looked confused, but Doug turned bright red. With that, Judy cried, "I know who!" and demanded that Keith kneel on one knee to propose, before leading them through their vows. Doug was clearly enjoying the scene, a big goofy smile never leaving his face, as Keith tried valiantly to regain his usual professorial composure.

Then came the big moment, as Judy pronounced them husband and wife—in the church of Judy-ism. "It's time for the kiss!" Judy announced. And the boys obliged.

Following in the footsteps of Al and Tipper Gore at the Democratic National Convention, Keith laid one on Doug. They pulled each other close, wrapped their arms around each other, and lip-locked passionately for a good minute and a half. The kiss in *Casablanca* should have *been* so steamy.

Were Keith and Doug sending a message to the audience? Perhaps. But it was crystal clear that they were sending a message to each other. A deeply penetrating message, at that.

Judy squealed, the audience mostly roared, and some of them looked away. My head was like an "ex-gay" in a gay porn store, looking back and forth, back and forth, from audience to Keith and Doug, audience to Keith and Doug.

"Look at that!" Judy cried. "Straight married couples usually go for a quick peck after seven years together. He's deep sea diving!" The audience laughed and clapped some more, and Keith pulled back from Doug, as they each smiled at the other. It was bliss on stage.

But why, you might ask, am I writing about a gay couple volunteering to go up on stage as the "married" couple in a suburban comedy club? The answer is simple, really. It's a sort of grass roots activism. Yup, just living your life proudly and happily is one of the most important forms of activism. The thing is, I don't think that Keith and Doug were thinking about that when they were on stage with Judy. They were just loving each other. And having fun along the way.

When we left the comedy club, we got shaken stares from some of the suburbanites, and thumbs up from others. Either way, their perspectives had been altered in a positive way.

And that's exactly as it should be.

DESIGNING MEN

A beautiful guy walks up to another man in a gay bar. He sidles up to the bar, positions himself to show off his big muscles and even bigger other attributes, and he says throatily, "Tonight is your lucky night. Buy me a few drinks, and I'll do anything you want." He flexes his biceps for added effect. The man at the bar looks him up and down, takes a sip of his drink, and replies, "Decorate my house."

Okay, I'll admit, it's an old straight joke adapted to a gay setting. But it's not that far off the mark. There are some stereotypes with a basis in reality. And with some exceptions, interior design ability seems to go hand in hand with being gay—way more than it does with being straight.

Not that there aren't plenty of exceptions to the rule. I should know, since I'm one of them. You see, I failed my first gay entrance exam. I love good food, but I can't cook. My culinary experiences can best be described as lab experiments in a kitchen, with only an occasional unidentifiable substance resulting from my efforts. ("These mashed potatoes are great, Kevin." "Thanks, but it's vanilla pudding.")

In the same way, I love great clothes, but I buy most of what I wear at Gap, or worse, Old Navy. (Morgan Fairchild and Magic the dog are good friends of mine.) I can't put a patterned tie with a striped shirt without serious fears of inadequacy. My mommy still sends me my ties.

And as for interior design, I have reasonably good taste, and I like look-ing at design magazines. *Architectural Digest, Southern Living*, even the occasional naughty-feeling peek at *Martha Stewart Living*. (How *does* she make a laundry room look like a boudoir at the Ritz? There must be some deep, dark evil afoot there, some sort of Faustian devil-in-the-decorating pact, because surely no mere human really lives that way? Sorry—I was having a Martha Stewart panic attack.) But while I enjoy looking at what other people do in their houses, if you ask me to choose a wallpaper to work with a border for the kitchen, I get a strange and helpless look on my face—like you'd just asked me to locate Cameron Diaz's G-spot. When it comes to the inside of my house, I'm more or less design-challenged. I can critique, but I can't create.

Yet I know loads of gay people, some of whom can't dress themselves in a reasonably cool way to save their lives, who can throw together a few odds and ends and make any apartment look fabulous. I should know. I dated one of them. His talents were one of the interesting—and frustrating—parts of our relationship.

When we first got together, he noticed that I had crystal candlesticks scattered throughout the apartment that I had accumulated over the years. He said, "Why don't you put them together in a collection? That will look good." So I did. I lined them up in order of size. From smallest to largest. He took one look and shook his head, waved his hands about like magic, and in a moment my candlestick line-up was an interesting, eye-catching collection of different sizes and shapes. Who knew?

One of the things he liked to do was to go to fabric stores. He dragged me along. I saw the pretty fabrics. I said, "Ooh." He got a studied look on his face, as he stroked the fabrics lovingly. He said, "This one here would be great for a throw pillow, if you re-upholstered your club chair in this other fabric there." I said, "Wow. You're right. How did you do that?"

It's not just fabrics, either. I like going antiquing (which seems to have caught on with the straight world these days, I would note). But when he was along, there was a whole new dimension: "An old, rusted wrought iron railing? Why, I'll spray it with fixative from the hardware store, put it up on the wall, and create an architectural look." Again, who knew? And it looked great over my candlesticks.

Sometimes when my boyfriend was around other gay men who have the same abilities, I felt rather intimidated. I felt almost like I should apologize—so sorry, but I just didn't get that gene. To compensate, I would periodically throw out pithy observations to prove that I was hip, too. Things like, "I really like blue," followed by a knowing nod.

But then, if you're around any group of straight men (without meaning to cast a negative stereotype), I don't think you'll find nearly as many men with the design talent. So while I didn't get the design gene myself that so many gay men seem to have, at least I can be proud that I'm part of a group of folks who excel in something I don't.

Martha Stewart can't hold a candle to our designing men.

WILL & GRACE UNDER PRESSURE

Until "Queer as Folk" hit cable, the biggest gay surprise of TV-land was NBC's *Will & Grace*. The show won both critical and viewer support in its first season (a rarity). It survived changes in time slot (another rarity). And it has a gay lead AND a way-gay key supporting role (yet another huge survival rarity). More importantly, it is bright and well-written (need I say how rare *that* is in sitcom TV?).

Among gay TV viewers, the show is a definite "love it" or "hate it" phenomenon. We love Will's sidekick Jack's over the top antics—sort of an *Ab Fab* goes queer. Jack is a walking advertisement for the fun, queeny (and sometimes funnily vacuous) side of gay culture—I'm surprised the religious right isn't all over him as a new gay recruitment ploy. Grace's sidekick Karen is walking attitude in a perfect body. One reviewer described her as "flamboyantly straight," the balance to Jack's "flamboyant gay" character. (Now there's a comparison you don't hear too often.) And Grace herself is a pretty, dingy red-head. (Shades of Lucy? *Literally?*)

The sticking point of the show for a lot of gay folks is Will. Will just isn't Willful enough. He's not zany enough. He's the gay leading man, but he's not gay enough. The fact that Will can't be everything gay for every gay man is enough to make a lot of gay men dislike the show.

Maybe those gay folks who dislike Will because he's not enough like Jack just can't handle the fact that Will is the comedic "straight man" on the team. No, I'm not talking about actor Eric McCormick's much-proclaimed heterosexuality. A classic aspect of comedy teamwork is the straight man—the average joe, the guy next door, the every-man that we identify with. The straight man gets to react and over-react (or in the case of Bob Newhart, under-react) to the nuttiness going on around him. The straight man usually has the dryest and wittiest lines. It is often his sub-tlety that cuts to the core. Costello had Abbott. Jerry Lewis had Dean Martin. Samantha had Darren. Dingy read-heads need their Cuban band leaders. (Take *that*, you *Will & Grace* haters.)

It's subtly ironic and just a little bit wicked that the straight man for this team is the gay man. Isn't it subversive that the calm, reassuring bit of normalcy for the viewers to identify with is a character they once might have called "deviant"?

Still, many gay folks stamp their feet and say, "But why can't Will be more like Jack?" And why can't he? Because Jack is a flighty queen with the depth of a birdbath. Sure, we all know someone like Jack. They're great fun, possibly really sweet deep down, but after any length of time they wear on your nerves like polyester. Two of them on one show would be too much.

The writers for *Will & Grace* are working to give Will more depth (and thus more character longevity). Will is a cute, quiet guy with a quick retort and a ready smile. He's deeply committed to the people he cares about. He sounds like a great friend, or the perfect boyfriend, now that they've done the Will-gets-over-his-internalized-homophobia episode.

This may actually be the true obstacle for the show to overcome. The writers have made Will the perfect friend for Grace. Now they seem to want to make the characters spend a lot of time agonizing over why they are such good friends. (Yawn.) We've all had friends where some spark drew you together, and the relationship just was. You don't question that kind of friendship. You revel in it. When the show revels, it soars. When it questions, it bogs down. It also smells slightly homophobic ("Maybe we can only be this close because we were meant to be a couple"—double yawn) and horribly angst-ridden. If I wanted angst, I'd be watching *Felicity*.

Perhaps soon, the writers will take enough of a breather to let go of that angst. (Just let it out, guys—breathe deeply now.) Maybe they'll focus on the wit that makes Will and Grace a modern Ricky and Lucy. Maybe they'll read this book.

In the meantime, I'll have to dream of another great sitcom, *Dharma & Greg*, splitting up. Hey, I can almost see *Will & Greg*...

GOT GAYDAR?

Got Gaydar? No, this is not a twisted version of the milk commercials. But it could be. Soon.

Gaydar, as any good gay person who's earned his or her recruitment toaster knows, is the mysterious, innate ability that gay folks generally have to tell if another person is gay. It's a sense that "I know he is" or "She's got Xena written all over her."

I've always thought it was based on the old concept of "it takes one to know one" (which was also the retort I used way back in high school when anyone called me queer—now I just say, "Yes, I am, but I'm not practicing anymore. I've got it perfected."). When your gaydar picks out someone in a room as gay, it's almost a subliminal sort of thing. The way he dresses, the way she walks, the way he talks, and—that most obvious clue of all—which butts her eyes follow.

But sometimes it's even more subtle than an interpretation of overt clues. Sometimes it's just a sense. The old "I had a feeling you were gay" reaction. I like to think of my gaydar as a special sort of electronic device—no, I did NOT say an electronic toy, and get your mind right back out of that gutter—that gives a "reading" on someone who is or might be gay. Sometimes it's a light reading. Melissa Etheridge and Anne Heche only gave me a blip, whereas George Michael and Ricky Martin shorted out the whole darned circuit.

It's a useful skill, not only for earning those recruitment bonus points (I jest—no need to recruit when the straight folks keep producing us, right?). It helps you find other members of the tribe, and that's a good feeling, since queer folks don't always come with a handy dandy Big Q on their foreheads for identification purposes.

But what of the natural gaydar-inhibited? Or worse, the entirely gaydar-challenged? I am talking of course about those poor besotted folks whose gaydar is not only broke, it's up on blocks in the side yard with the wheels off. You know who I'm talking about. The friend who couldn't tell another guy was gay if he showed up in a Carmen Miranda outfit and offered to show him a big banana.

Well, for these folks there is now hope. A British company called Borer's Nest has introduced a new product billed as—you guessed it—"Gaydar ™, the World's First Portable Interactive Matchmaker for the Lesbian and Gay Community." "Gaydar—the Gay Radar ™", according to the company's website, is a "small key chain device that…answers the questions 'Is he queer? or 'Is she attached?' The Gaydar informs you if a gay person is within 30 feet of you, and then you can easily introduce yourselves."

The device depends upon another gay person carrying another unit in switched on position, so it won't become terribly practical until a lot of people start to purchase the product. But once they do, whether you're walking down the street or sitting in a subway car, if there's another gay person nearby, your unit will beep, flash, and possibly vibrate (your choice) to let you know. According to the company, the best part is that no extra effort is required. "Gaydar creates an immediate common ground, and of course a topic of conversation to break the ice with."

Scary, ain't it?

I usually operate on a simple maxim: "If it ain't broke, don't fix it." This applies to computers, boyfriends, and, yes, even gaydar. My own internal gaydar works pretty well generally, except of course with Europeans and some Latinos. Most Europeans are culturally queer anyway. I mean, really—between men kissing men hello, women holding hands or arm in arm as they walk down the street, and just a trace of macho mixed in with that all that sensitivity in the men—my gaydar starts going off like poppers at a Circuit Party. (Thank goodness Jerry Falwell, a.k.a. the Tinkmaster, doesn't live in Europe. He'd be pointing fingers not just at Tinky Winky but at the inhabitants of the whole doggone continent as well.)

Besides, I don't know if I could handle a device that could start flashing, beeping, and possibly vibrating in my trousers at inconvenient moments. Like when you're going through the security checkpoint at airports. With all those gay flight attendants buzzing around, the thing would be going to town. And there's nothing like approaching security personnel when your pants pocket starts to shimmy.

More to the point, I don't think I'll be getting a gaydar unit for a more basic reason: I'm not the most coordinated person in the world. (My Indian name is "Runs With Scissors.") I don't know if I could handle all the buttons on such a little device. Walking and talking on a cell phone is already a challenge for me, though it is a nice way to run into new people—literally. How would I ever re-calibrate my gaydar on the fly?

So while I may not be buying into the upcoming Got Gaydar? campaign, I'll be watching others more closely now for those tell-tale flashing, beeping, and quite possibly vibrating trousers. The wonders of technology will never cease.

Who knew gaydar was next?

THE GAY ART OF THE GIFT

On a recent trip to visit my parents, Mom and I went shopping together—which, I often point out, is one of the perks of having a gay son. She showed me a very chic evening gown she had really wanted to buy. Unfortunately, no store in town had the right color in the right size. She even tried on the dress in another color so I could see how fabulous it was.

It was time to do the gay son thing. When she went back into the fitting room, I asked the store clerk to write down all the information that I would need to find the dress in a department store when I returned home. Boy, would Mom be surprised for Mother's Day.

Well, let me tell you, when I dragged my boyfriend kicking and screaming into the "Social Dresses" section of seven department stores, I realized that this quest was not nearly as easy as I had expected it would be. Worse yet, the women shopping in the evening dresses section really tend to stare at a guy rifling through racks of gowns. I felt like yelling at some of them, "Do I LOOK like a size six to YOU?! This is NOT for me!" But in the seventh store, just as I was about to give up, there it was—and better yet, it was on sale!

Then I had to stand in a line of ten women waiting to make my purchase, all the while thinking, "Standing here in line holding a silver ball gown with all these women and men staring at me—this has to be worth another few months of therapy..." But I should get major gay son brownie points when I give Mom her gift. Now I just have to get it to her without crushing, wrinkling or otherwise maiming the thing. My prior experience with evening gowns is, admittedly, limited.

Therapy aside, that's part of the fun of finding the right gifts to give to the important people in your life. And not that I want to draw stereotypes, but it seems to me that gay men are generally better gift givers than their straight male counterparts. For years I've heard my straight best friend moan in dismay over the gifts that her boyfriends have given her. Several rather hideous necklaces comes to mind, apparently from the late Flintstones collection. "What was he thinking?" are words I've heard many a time. (For the record, she's finally in a relationship where the guy has a really nice gift box.)

Last Christmas, my dad surprised me with an unusual gift. A toaster. Yes, that thing that toasts the bread and bagels for breakfast in the morning. Unfortunately, I prefer to use the cute little guy down at the coffee shop for that. Besides, I already have a toaster that I got when I reached my gay recruitment quota last year.

Not that Dad's toaster wasn't very nice in an expensive, multi-function sort of way. You know how straight men are about electronic gadgets. Sort of like lesbians and power tools. My sister is just now learning this little fact of life, dealing with her new husband's obsession with things electronic and powerful, particularly items from the Bob Vila collection. As a result, she is rapidly training my brother-in-law—in loud, not uncertain terms—that such items are not acceptable as gifts for her.

When it comes to the gift giving arena, I think the main difference between straight men and gay men is that gay men generally listen to the people they're trying to buy gifts for. We know enough about the people to try to gauge their tastes, and we try to buy things that we know they would really like to have. Any boyfriend of mine, for instance, certainly realizes that kitchen appliances and car maintenance books will buy him quite a few cold, lonely nights.

So yet again, gay men are one step ahead of straight men. Our gift giving skills—are they environmental or genetic?—are second to none. As Mom often points out to her friends, there are perks to having a gay son.

Lead or Follow.
Stereotypes Just Can't Boogie

THE PERILS OF A GAY HOME BUYER

Finding a house to buy is a lot like finding a boyfriend or girlfriend. When you finally find one you like, the first thing you do is try to change it.

When I finally paid off my last student loan recently, I decided that it was time for me to put down roots. Or at least come up with some other large debt that I can use to fill the gaping emptiness in my life where my student debt used to be. Besides, there's only so much you can do with an apartment, and even though my gay design genes are limited at best, I am a great organizer. I like projects and plans. And I've re-organized one too many boyfriend's closets. ("Order out of chaos," I said. *You labeled my socks and divided them by color,*" he replied in shock.)

The first thing I did when I decided to take the plunge into the turbulent waters of buying a place was to find a real estate agent. A family oriented agent, that is. I needed someone who would understand my special concerns about living space. Proximity to the gayer areas of town is important to me. Easy access to restaurants, movies, and my favorite coffee house are key. I'm not looking for a house in the extreme suburbs, no matter how affordable it might be, and I am definitely not into major yard work. I got enough of that when I was growing up. (I learned to drive on a riding lawnmower.)

Ultimately, for the choice of agents, it was a toss-up between a tough-as-nails lesbian (did you see the movie *The Negotiator?*) and a gay man with construction experience. My lesbian friend is an exception to the stereotype of lesbians and power tools, and I'm looking for a fixer-upper (again, isn't it just like dating?), so I decided to go with the guy with construction experience. Unlike some gay folks, I don't walk into a house and say, "That wall must go!" My skills do not extend that far, and I was terrible at Tinker Toys. I needed the remodeling advice.

Once we started looking, I realized that finding the right house or condo—or humble hovel—wasn't going to be as easy as I thought. You see, there are two basic types of existing homeowners. The gay or lesbian, and the handicapped, otherwise known as straight.

Almost every place you look at that is owned by gay folks is move-in quality. Crown molding, fabulous kitchens, up-dated bathrooms (gotta love those two-headed showers), open, airy, and bright. (Not unlike my last boyfriend after I'd completed his re-training and released him back into the dating pool.) But the houses built by gay folks are priced to match. Then there are the ones owned by the artsy or frou-frou gay folks. The ones with the koi ponds beside the patio and the dog house with the miniature marble staircase. This is where the gene goes too far.

It's a whole other experience when you look at homes owned by straight folks. The difference is sometimes astonishing. It's a lot like being in the movie *The Wizard of Oz* and going back to Kansas. Everything goes from techni-color to black and white. I find myself wondering, "How do these people live this way? Is it environmental or genetic?" There are kitchens in need of a wrecking ball, hideous carpets covering perfectly good hardwood floors, and wallpapers that would make a cannibal queasy.

I have developed a coping mechanism to adapt to the shock of looking at such places. First, I walk in and gasp in initial shock and dismay. Then I close my eyes, click my heels together three times, and repeat, "There's nothing like crown molding, there's nothing like crown molding!" Buying a straight-owned home is a little like dating a guy direct from his parents' farm in Iowa. There may be a lot of potential there, but a lot of work has to go into it. And I'm just not into complete reconstruction. I am not a lesbian.

Still, I've learned to look at a place and immediately imagine it as I would want it to be. And in a way, that's the same approach I've always taken to life as a gay person. I look at things the way they are, and I imagine them the way I want them to be. Then I just do it.

Maybe someday I'll be a happy homo homeowner. If I survive the perils of house hunting, I'll be putting up crown molding soon.

WELCOME TO WAFFLE HOUSE

As queer folks, we're known around the world for our discriminating tastes. Whether it's clothes or interior design or food, we're usually on the cutting edge, leading the way, and well ahead of the curve. But sometimes I've just got to take a detour.

Why, you might ask? Well, I'm glad you did. Have you ever noticed that a number of the most fashionable places seem to serve dishes that offer you a convenient way to starve? And for big bucks, at that. In those restaurants, it's true that size matters. But it seems to be the opposite of what you want with a guy. Apparently, the smaller the entrée, the better it is. By way of simple comparison, I have a mental image of saying to a fellow, "Nope. Sorry. Too big. Can I send you back for a smaller size?" Somehow I just can't see that happening. (I, for one, will never discriminate against large men. They deserve our support, and we should stand behind them. Or in front of them.)

Yet, despite the apparent absurdity, it appears that the chefs at the fabulously chic restaurants have exactly that idea. I can just hear one now. "Oh, no, Jean-Claude! Oh, la, la! You are ruining the presentation! I need to see more plate—more PLATE, you idiot—and less *filet de langue de boeuf sautee dans une sauce de cerises!*" So you end up getting a lovely dish that would easily double as a centerpiece. At the kindergarten table.

But these very places are often flocked to by gay men in the food fashion patrol. Or more precisely, the cuisine brigade. You see, when you get to that level, it's not food anymore. It's cuisine. Somehow everything sounds better in French. Even potatoes boiled in oil—and if I'm not mistaken, boiling in oil was once a medieval torture—sound better when they're called French fries.

Granted, we're not always in *nouvelle cuisine* mode, and we usually pick restaurants with the best atmosphere, too. There's nothing like being in a restaurant surrounded by attractive, well-dressed men and women enjoying their own company. Cute guys laughing. Sexy women exchanging glances. Good music, good service (there's no denying that gay and lesbian waitrons are the best in the world), and good food. It's a recipe for a great queer evening. And, interestingly enough, gay folks always find the best new restaurants centuries before they're discovered by straights. We have the nose that knows. (Possibly because it's been in different places than the hetero counterpart.)

But I must confess that every now and then, I have an urge to take a detour. To boldly go where millions of truck drivers and un-washed yuppies in college sweats have gone before. To seek out new life and new civilizations, or at least a Dunk'N Dine, or a Waffle House, or whatever the local equivalent of a greasy spoon diner is. A place where you can wear shorts and a baseball cap to cover the bed-head you woke up with, as you slurp barely okay coffee and peruse the slightly stained menu.

Yes, it's weekend morning nirvana, if you're not feeling chic enough for the local queer-frequented coffee house or bagel shop. Maybe your tan is feeling faded and your hair is plastered down with goo to make it look less like the bird's nest you woke up with. And you're looking over a menu that includes items like "biscuits baked with freshest lard" or "eggs scrambled in day-old bacon grease." "Hmm," you think. "How do I want my cholesterol and fat intake today? Maybe hash browns smothered, covered, scattered, or chunked? How about all of the above!" After all, sometimes a break from health consciousness seems like the healthiest thing you can do.

Besides, there's a certain camp element to diners that appeals to a queer sensibility. I like the fact the waitresses have been there for a thousand years. I am comforted by the reasonable certainty that her name is probably Ethel or Josephine. (You'll note that they're almost never named Daphne. Or Brittany. Or even Buffy.) And I admire the skill required in getting hair that big. After all, we all know in the South that the higher your hair, the closer you are to God. In a diner, the waitress is the queen, and you're nothing but a princess. Which is exactly as it should be.

So whenever you're feeling a strong urge to abandon the cool queer restaurant scene for something a little more, well, back-to-nature, it's perfectly okay to exchange your royalty status with Ethel, the grandmotherly waitress with the grease-stained apron. The one who says, "Hey there, Honey. How ya doin'? Welcome to Waffle House!"

THE GOLD STANDARD

I loved the ad. Two attractive, smiling men comfortably ensconced on a sofa. In front of them, a smiling toddler in her own little chair. The caption: "A kid deserves to feel at home." I immediately wondered, "Can I buy the whole set? Or just the furniture?"

Seriously though, the men behind the furniture—and the ad—are just as interesting themselves. Gay partners Mitchell Gold and Bob Williams are the driving force behind Mitchell Gold furniture—the thrust beneath the seats, if you will. A few years ago, Gold realized that clothing designers were selling scads of high priced men's underwear—the unglamorous necessities of male life that used to be associated, coincidentally, with talking fruits and snappy elastic waist bands—by using beefcake models and provocative ads.

No one else in the furniture industry was using advertising in any similar way, unless of course you counted those comfortably large middle-aged men reclining languidly in their barcoloungers. So Gold, whose furniture operations, along with his home with his partner are in North Carolina, decided that he could do the same with the advertising for his line of moderately priced furniture. From strategically covered men on sofa-sleepers, to the ad with the two men and the little girl, Gold's ads have attracted attention to his furniture. And along with name recognition have come sales.

As I thought about this object lesson in pure capitalism with a gay bent, I began to wonder. How many other gay or lesbian partners are out there running their own successful businesses? And, I wondered, what sort of creative ad campaigns could they use? Being the creative type that I am (read: too much time on my hands?), I came up with a list of possible products and ads, just in case Mitchell Gold should ever decide to expand its offerings. Because unless you're talking the federal deficit, waist or thighs, expansion is a good thing, right?

First, you have to have a place to keep all that great furniture. Picture two men working happily on This Old Gay House. "Every bolt deserves a good-fitting nut." Or two women joyfully trimming the shrubbery. "A power tool for every need." Then picture two men building their own wine cellar. "Because every man needs a reliable drill."

Then we move from hardware to software. Like textiles. Two beautiful women sprawl comfortably on an Oriental rug. "Our carpets will always match your drapes."

A tall, handsome man lowers his muscular, shirtless partner onto pillows by the fire. "Tough AND soft."

More and more ads come to mind, each involving sexy models. Do it yourself tile. "Always an easy lay." Furniture care products. "Just rub it on, then rub it off." Paint and varnish remover. "Easy to strip." Spa baths. "Something to slip into." Wallpaper. "Obviously well hung."

Things are getting out of hand. Let's consider other markets. Maybe sports equipment. Picture two hunky baseball players—male or female, take your pick. "Every pitcher deserves a good catcher." Or maybe two muscular women in football gear. "Because sometimes a regular pad just isn't enough." The ad possibilities are endless: balls and bats, the perfect basket, he shoots he scores, etc.

How about pets and pet care. Definitely a gay market. Picture two men and a Dalmatian frolicking in the park. "Collars, leashes, muzzles—maybe even something for your dog." Then two women with two very content cats. "Always remember to wash, pet, and stroke your..." Well, maybe not.

What about clothes? We shouldn't forget that market. Imagine two men in briefs playing tug of war with a pair of blue jeans. "It's great when you know you can get into his pants." Or maybe two women helping each other slip out of their flannel. "It's not often you'll get this shirt off of her back."

And then there's sleepwear. Offered by catalog. Victoria's Secret meets Tool Time. Or International Male meets, well, International Male. The ad slogan: "With our pajamas, all our tops fit all our bottoms. Mix and match. Because every top deserves a great bottom."

Maybe I'm getting a little too carried away with this whole sexy ad campaign stuff. It's not as if Mitchell Gold has gone completely over the top. His ads are always sexy but tasteful. I guess I'll have to come up with ads for something with less sex appeal. How about the U.S. Postal Service? I've got the perfect stamp ad. "Just lick it and stick it."

SCOUTS ON THE ROCKS

"Don't the Boy Scouts of America know how many Eagle Scouts are gay? *Please.* If I had a feather for every one I've ever gone on a date with, I'd have a headdress to put Bob Mackie to shame."

That was my first thought when I read about the court case permitting the Boy Scouts of America to discriminate against gay boys and men in their ranks. My second thought was to recall the Scout law. "A Scout is trustworthy, loyal, helpful, friendly, courteous, kind, obedient, cheerful, thrifty, brave, clean, and reverent." Which, I believe, describes your average gay man quite nicely. (Except for the "obedient" part, of course, which only applies if it's consensual and enjoyable for both partners.)

I thought that would be the end of the matter. The phrase "morally straight" (as opposed to "immorally gay"?) in the Boy Scout oath didn't leave room for gay folks in that group. The Scouts won the right to discriminate. Case closed.

But my, my, what a difference a Supreme Court ruling makes. And it's not always the one you were expecting. Sometimes it's almost—well—downright subversive. Scout's honor.

You see, since the Supreme Court upheld the Boy Scouts of America's right to discriminate against gay scouts and leaders, some rather surprising things have been happening. And despite their motto, I don't think the Scouts were prepared. I know I wasn't.

That giant snapping sound you've been hearing all over this great country of ours is the sound of money purses slapping shut—to the Boy Scouts of America, that is. Why, I'm so tickled, I could tie a slip knot, which I still remember from my days as a Cub Scout. Chicago and San Francisco have closed their parks and schools to local Scout troops. Connecticut has banned contributions to the Scouts by state employees through state-run charities. Chase Manhattan Bank stopped contributing its $200,000 annually to the Scouts. And they're only the tip of the kerchief.

Meanwhile, Scouting for All, a group started by a 15-year-old scout in California that advocates opening up the organization to gay folks, is protesting in cities around the country. Parents who do not agree with the anti-gay policy are standing up and voicing their opposition. And there is a move in the U.S. Congress to revoke the largely symbolic federal charter of the Boy Scouts of America. Well, just slap me upside the head with a pup tent. Who knew this was coming?

Syndicated New York columnist Maggie Gallagher—writers are not by and large the most attractive lot, and Ms. Gallagher is proof of that assertion—complains that gay activists are hurting kids by "bullying" the Boy Scouts of America. Aw, break my heart some more, Maggie! (And while you're at it, get a gay Eagle Scout to do something about your hair.)

Let's try this again, Maggie, and all the others out there like you (bad hair and mean-spirited). What do you call a huge organization that tells a young kid, "You can't be part of our club if you're gay"? Yes, that's right. A bully. The Boy Scouts are telling gay kids, "You're wrong for being gay." When the kids are not wrong. The Scouts are. If that's not "bullying," I don't know what is.

Of course, the most effective way to deal with a bully is to fight back. And since money talks, that's a great place to start. What can you do to help keep those purses snapping shut? It's pretty simple, and relatively non-threatening. If you work for a company with that gives charitable gifts, and you have a non-discrimination clause that says your company doesn't discriminate on the basis of sexual orientation, then try sending a friendly little email to your HR director. I did.

Something like, "Should our company (which doesn't discriminate) be giving money to the Boy Scouts of America (which does discriminate)? That would seem inconsistent. Sort of like giving money to a group that discriminates against Jews, women, or African-Americans, which I am certain we would never, ever do. Just a thought." Love ya, mean it, blah, blah, blah. You don't even have to self-identify as gay, if you're not particularly out at work.

It's just a simple question. And surprisingly, it's often a simple question that brings results.

Scout's honor.

Disco.
I Love the Night Life

THAT 70'S GUY

If I see another pair of bell bottom blue jeans, I think I'm going to have to ring somebody's bell.

The 70's are upon us in a big way. It started out innocently enough. A few retro shirts at the GAP. A few midriff baring tops on waif-like girls (and some gay boys). Calvin Klein ran some creepy ads with eerily adolescent models. Then before you knew it, there was "That 70's Show" on the tube and—the utter horror of it—"Saturday Night Fever," a faithful re-do of the John Travolta movie, opening to sold-out audiences on Broadway.

As usual, the style setter of the world (queer folks—who else?) were already on the bandwagon. At first I thought it might be limited to the Circuit Party set, who are trend setters in and of themselves, appearing in striped, skin-tight track pants and those damnably ugly M*A*S*H style fishing hats (which was a little like watching MacLain Stevenson with a great chest). Hair was cut short in early 70's G.I. fashion, and sometimes dog tags even bounced on glistening chests as men danced.

Then I noticed the younger set. The hair was longer, in late 70's fashion. But that wasn't the end of it. If you look around, you'll notice that practically every gay boy under the age of 25 is wearing hip hugger jeans on hips that are barely big enough to hug. You see, part of 70's fashion was the thin, "natural" body type. Tom of Finland, it ain't. Sometimes when I drive past the teen hang out at the queer bookstore, I feel like throwing emergency bacon cheeseburgers at them. And you can forget flannel on the girls. Try ribbed tanks and navel rings. Butch and burly lesbians seem to have been superseded by the slinky and slightly emaciated (in a sullen, sultry, "please feed me" sort of way).

Perhaps the most interesting twist on this influx of 70's looks is the inherent conflict it creates. For so long, we've all seen the gym body as the ideal look. "No pecs, no sex" and all that jazz. Now we're seeing something entirely alien to the gym set—the skinny and lean look.

And this is all having an interesting side effect, which I call "gay carbon dating." As I mentioned, the younger crowd is all about 70's skinny and lean. The beefy, muscled types are by and large over the age of 25, and in many cases well over 30 and beyond. They're dating themselves, and they don't even know it. For a youth obsessed culture, we're a little slow getting on the clue bus here. Could it be that "beefy and built" now translates into "old"? Yeesh! Beam me up, Voyager!

Of course, I happen to like a well-shaped chest and arms, so I'd probably go for "older" most days. But I've been moderating my own work outs of late, and maybe I'm not alone in that. Maybe the 70's trend will have a moderating influence on the gym obsession of recent years. Between the waif and the beef lies the healthily buffed and lean. Which would fill out those hip huggers and midriff tops nicely, thank you.

The scary thing is that my fashion friends tell me that styles recycle ever twenty years or so. Thus, in the 90's and early 00's, we've re-vamped the 70's. Do you know what that means? Soon there will be a return to—egads!—the 80's.

Can you say "preppie dearest"? Pink and green? Up-collar polo shirts? Oh, God, the horror! Somebody shoot me! Or at least swat me with a squash racquet! I've already seen a couple of fashion forward guys out and about in shorts and sweater sets. I just don't know if I can handle a decade of slicked back hair, power suits, and those annoying little polo men riding across my shirts. Not to mention neon bike shorts. (Imagine them on overweight straight men, the kind who God-only-knows-why thinks every gay man is attracted to them. Talk about an image from hell.) It'll be tough to face the 80's coming round again.

For now, though, we've still got the 70's, and I will survive. I fully intend to enjoy the remaining year(s) of 70's style. The V-necked tight shirts. The stripes on the arms. The tight track pants. The flat, bare midriffs.

You gotta love that 70's gay guy and gal.

It's My Party

As Ms. Behavior might tell you in her pointedly funny way, it is never proper to ask a lady for her age. And if you ask a gay man his age—then heaven have pity on your soul.

Birthdays, after the age of thirty or so, usually inspire a sense of dread, or at least profound distaste and the occasional gagging spell—gagging anyone who might be about to spill the beans on your age, that is. Sure, there's the hope of getting lots of cards with scantily clad, buffed men on the covers, for that extra lift to get you through. But one crack about—well, your expanding Joe-the-plumber crack—brings you right back to reality.

Yet sometimes birthdays and their associated hoopla and merriment are actually exciting events. We all need some celebration now and again. And every now and then, there's a really special birthday party, like the one for my friend Jesse.

You see, Jesse was diagnosed with HIV fifteen years ago. Yes, fifteen. He continued to practice as a head shrink (his term, not mine) for another seven years. But then eight years ago when his health worsened, he retired to take better care of himself and to live out his remaining time. Basically, he was setting off on an uncertain ride into the sunset.

Jesse continued to live his life, of course, socializing with his large circle of friends and taking periodic trips to New York City for a healthy dose of Broadway. And there have always been the weekly summer poolside gatherings at his house. These are pleasant reunions of writers, doctors, waiters, and other varied sorts, many of whom doff their swimsuits for the *au naturel* look. (Hey, I don't like tan lines. On a pale blond like me, they look like dirt lines.)

And as we discuss our lives and politics and advances in AIDS treatments and who's dating whom, Jesse keeps a watchful eye out over his two dogs, who have learned to play Lifeguard with me. These surfing minischnauzers jump onto rafts the minute I prepare to dive, and they bark and bite at the waves, tails wagging furiously, trying to save me from the water I'm jumping into. (Jump. Rinse. Repeat. You get the picture.) They're sort of like their dad in the giving aid department.

Because despite his own circumstance, Jesse threw his time and money into more AIDS service groups (even founded a couple) than I would have thought possible for a man of his health. But Jesse is not just any PLWA (that's "Person LIVING With AIDS," thank you very much), nor any ordinary person, for that matter. As a trained physician himself with broad connections (clearly, those wild parties in the '70s paid off), Jesse threw himself into AIDS aid. Heck, he was even instrumental in the funding and building of the first AIDS memorial park in town. I remember when he was selling those engraved paving stones to raise money for the park— the high pressure sales tactics, the Mafia-style arm-twisting, the begging and pleading—it was worse than Girl Scout Cookie season.

At the time he retired, Jesse hoped to live to see the 1996 Olympics. Living to see the advent of the Millennial celebrations was beyond his wildest imaginings. But last week he turned 60, and he's healthier now than he's been in years.

So it was time for a party, with revelry, laughter, and colorful accessories. Mardi Gras seemed the only appropriate theme. The party brought together all sorts of people who care about Jesse, from his minister (who told the foulest joke I've ever heard a man of the cloth tell) to party boys in mesh shirts and tightly stretched leather.

Inevitably, the party turned into a bit of a roast, led by a drag queen emcee named Bubba D. Licious (a Southern drag queen). One of Jesse's

Army buddies, from the pre-don't-ask-don't-tell days, told of how he and Jesse once came upon an elderly woman who had stranded herself by locking her keys in her car. With a gay man's expertise with tools, Jesse jimmied the lock with a coat hangar in no time flat. The surprised and grateful woman asked, "What line of work are you boys in?" To which Jesse responded with a courtly bow and the reply, "We're professional car thieves, ma'am, and today is our day off."

Forty years later, Jesse is still helping people, only this time it's people with a virus instead of a car problem. And he still has his quirky sense of humor. That's probably why I like him as much as I do.

But the thing I reminded myself, as I sat laughing through the party, is that Jesse is not alone out there. Sometimes we gay folks may forget that there are a whole host of other gays and lesbians out there doing amazing things with their lives even in the face of AIDS. And these people deserve our notice and applause. You could say they even deserve a party.

I'm just looking forward to Jesse's 70th.

IN SEARCH OF GAY BERLIN

There's not much left of the Berlin Wall these days. Checkpoint Charlie (which, in my opinion, always sounded like the name of a gay disco) actually checked out years ago. And the Iron Curtain has been replaced with a lovely see-through sheer.

I wasn't sure what to expect from a visit to Berlin. About all I know how to say in German is "May I have coffee and apple strudel, please?" Which pretty much covers the important bases, in my view, since I'm a sucker for good coffee and gooey pastries.

Still, I kept trying to imagine the gay Berlin of the 1920s, the wild city with more than 300 gay and lesbian establishments that disappeared under a short, mustachioed madman's boot. But since the fall of the Wall, Berlin has come a long way, baby. Much to my surprise, Berlin now has more gay bars, clubs, restaurants, and cafes than you can shake a wiener-schnitzel at. It ranks second only after Amsterdam as the place for gay and lesbian night life in Europe.

The Germans themselves are an interesting bunch. I haven't seen that many men wearing leather pants since I accidentally crashed a Siegfried and Roy look-a-like contest. But if you like mostly blond (often very dirty blond, both in terms of color AND daily hair hygiene) and light-eyed men, Berlin is the city for you. And I particularly love the way the Germans always obey the rules. At a street crossing, no one will start walking across the street until the little green man lights up—even if there is no one coming for kilometers. I can only imagine how useful this characteristic could be in the bedroom, where following orders can REALLY be fun. They're every leather daddy's dream.

Speaking of hot fun, Berlin is actually a great place to SHOP. The city even has the largest department store on the Continent. Opened after the fall of the Wall, KaDeWe (yes, it's pronounced "kah-dee-wee"—say it three times fast and you'll sound like Meg Ryan in that classic *When Harry Met Sally* scene) has just about anything you could possibly want. It's a Martha Stewart queen's dream. From crystal to clothes to funky bed linens, you can relax and go slow, working yourself into a state of pure bliss. This store is truly fabulous, which is a word I never typically associate with department stores. Only apple strudel.

In addition to having the largest department store on the Continent, it turns out that Berlin is the largest construction zone in Europe. There are hard hats, not to mention large tools, just about everywhere. It's like an explosion of the Village People, only without the Indian. Huge swaths of the former East Berlin are building sites. With most of the city destroyed during the Second World War, much of Berlin's Old World charm was lost, but the city is being rebuilt as a 21st century European city. With all the power tools everywhere, it's a lesbian's dream.

In the evening, there are plenty of choices in places to eat, but perhaps the most fun restaurant in Berlin turned out, predictably, to be one in the gay area of town. LukiLuki is pronounced "Look-ee, look-ee." There's a reason for that. The restaurant's food, which is good (who knew the Germans could make good escargot to go with that sauerkraut), is not the main attraction. That is because all of the servers are either drag queens or shirtless muscle boys. Look-ee, look-ee, indeed. The only problem I had was that they couldn't understand when I kept asking, "Can I get HIM on the menu?" That following orders thing just wasn't working.

So now I guess I'll have to learn a few basic commands in German before I get back to Berlin again. (I have a friend who trains his Doberman in the language. Commands like "Sit!", "Beg!", and "Roll over!" seem like useful things to know.)

Next time I'm in Berlin, I'll be prepared.

BIG GAY PRIDE

Once a year, something really, really big comes upon us.

Yes, it's Pride season across the land. The time of year when we queer folks of every size, shape, color, and brief-or-boxer preference come together to celebrate ourselves.

And each year, we have even more to be proud of. This year we salute ourselves, our gay ambassadors, our queer elected officials, our queer entertainers, and everyone else livin' la vida loca—er, gay.

Most of the Pride Parades across the USA happen during the summer months, marking the anniversary of the Stonewall Riots, which happened on the heels of gay icon Judy Garland's death. You would have thought that Judy could have had a little more consideration for her gay fans than to pass on right in the middle of summer. I mean, really—late June!? Couldn't she have gone in balmy May or September? Especially for the sake of the Southern queers who suffer in often unbearable heat. But then, maybe she was being considerate in another way. After all, I'm not gonna complain about the cute shirtless guys.

I look forward to the marching groups from the Human Rights Campaign, the gay business groups, the AIDS groups, everyone being incredibly visible in an out-there parade. It's the one time of year where we see so many of our fellow queers and make the ever-so-important statement, "We are not alone!" We're here, we're queer, and we're gonna have a good time!

I look forward to seeing the rainbow colored floats and the bright costumes—and the inevitable contingent of bare breasted lesbians swangin' to and fro. From a gay man's perspective, since we don't see those twin critters too often, it's kind of like being in a live National Geographic special, only without those disturbing heterosexual overtones.

And then, of course, there are the drag queens. I used to dislike the prominent presence of drag queens in Pride parades, because you could bet that the news coverage would broadcast pictures of ONLY drag queens, which I suppose made the rest of America comfortable in thinking that all gays wore dresses and fab make-up. I guess it was a way the straight folks could identify us without having to tag us first and release us back into the wild. ("Look, little Johnny. Do you see that man in the glam MAC make-up and the Donna Karan gown? That's a gay person.")

I "used to" dislike the prominence of drag queens at Pride parades, because I quickly realized that (a) the excess coverage was the media's fault, not the drag queens', (b) if I thought that way, I was engaging in the very same discrimination we were fighting, and (c) drag queens with lesbians started the whole Stonewall riots, so they deserve their moment of fabulousness. Besides, they're funny and fun, and isn't that what Pride should be?

In the larger cities, Pride Parades seem to be evolving into a more entertaining, Mardi Gras style spectacle. Let's face it: in New York, Boston, San Francisco and Atlanta, the general population pretty much already knows we're here and we're queer. They're used to it already. While the political banners are ever more important, so is the pure celebration of pride, community and fun together and with our non-queer friends and family.

After all, Mardi Gras, or Fat Tuesday, began as a religious event marking the last day of revelry before the beginning of Lent, a period of fasting and prayer. Mardi Gras evolved from its religious beginnings into a huge, colorful, and sometimes outrageous celebration. Maybe Pride will evolve that way, too. As a group, we're awfully darn creative and talented, and we can put on one hell of a show. (Move over Ricky Martin. Get a load of THIS!)

I can imagine rainbow crewes, at least one for each color in the flag, competing to out do each other with their floats. There would be an I Love Judy float to commemorate the beginning of it all. Maybe a Tom of Finland float and a Xena the Warrior Princess chariot. Big Gay Al and the Simpson's Mr. Smithers could be the cartoon blow-up dolls floating up above.

Hey, it could happen. That's the great thing about big things. Sometimes they just keep getting bigger.

Dirty Dancin'.
When Clean is NOT an Option

SAFER DATING 101

Every now and then, I feel compelled to make a public service announcement. On a useful subject. Like dating.

So without further ado, here are a few basic dating rules for the single-and-looking. (Disclaimer: For the single-and-playing-around, these rules do not apply, because love-'em-and-leave-'em is a totally different game.)

Rule Number One. Avoid guys with intricate past dating dramas. If he describes more than one ex-boyfriend as a "stalker"—and there is more than one restraining order involved—then just walk on by. If you find yourself thinking, "He's so charming and sweet. He must have just had a string of really bad luck with men"—then your next thought should be, "If I get involved with this guy, I'll be the one he's talking about on his next date." So run. Don't walk. Run. Remember the old Southern adage, "You can take the trash out of the trailer, but you can't take the trailer out of the trash." And a restraining order just doesn't look good on your resume.

Rule Number Two. Beware of the Hallmark Card Company poster guy. Sure, cards are wonderful. Flowers are delightful. Candy is divine. Too much, too soon of any of them—or worse, in combination—is a recipe for disaster. But why, you might ask? After all, he likes me, he really likes me! Well, there are two reasons, Sunshine. First, he's probably allowed himself to be so mistreated in the past that he thinks you are a god—and he's going to have serious self-esteem issues that go hand in hand with someone who's let himself be mistreated. Second, he's subjecting you to the Vanna White syndrome, where he doesn't really know you, but he's projecting everything he wants in a guy on to the little bit of you—and maybe the fabulous dresses—he's had time to see so far. But it's a long, hard fall from the pedestal he's put you on. Think Humpty Dumpty. And you won't even get to enjoy all the king's horses—or all the king's men.

Rule Number Three. Stay away from men who keep you at arm's length. To quote a Dutch friend of mine, "If you can't see the crack in the dyke, don't expect the water to come surging through." Wait a minute. That was a Dutch *lesbian* friend of mine. And I'm not sure she was talking about sea walls. But the principle is the same. If you're looking for anything more than casual dating, you have to see some signs within a reasonable amount of time that the guy you like is interested in more, too. Don't waste your time thinking, "He'll warm up to me. I need to give him time." Because it's not going to happen. The important thing to consider is where you and he are in being ready for a relationship with someone—not where he could be in six months. I'm not saying you should drop all barriers on the first date. But if the motor's not revving on the tenth pass around the track, then, honey, it's time to get a new set of wheels. Or at least pay closer attention to that pit crew.

Rule Number Four. Always ask questions about his current relationship status. Ask whether he has a partner. If he says no, ask if he is living with anyone, and if yes, whether he and the roommate have ever, at any time in the past, dated or had more than friendly feelings for each other. I know it sounds like the third degree, but you'd be amazed at how many guys out there will find creative ways to two-time a significant other. And when you ultimately find out the truth, they'll say, "But you never asked!" What this means is, "You never asked the right question." Now, this is not a gay thing. It's a Y chromosome thing. So pretend your Perry Gayson and cross examine your witness up front. You'll save yourself some heartache. And the added embarrassment of sharing that Whitman's Sampler on Valentine's Day.

Herewith, we conclude our presentation of the Rules of Safer Dating. So with this advice in hand, go forth and multiply. Or at least have fun trying.

This Dating Public Service Announcement has been brought to you by the Society for Curing Unpleasant Men (SCUM) and the Gay Alliance for Great Male Experiences (GAG ME).

DOT.GAY

When you think of "the internet," do images of glorious hordes of dot.com's romp through your head? Or do you think "geek-o-rama"? Probably not, on both counts. Though some of you may have thought "sex-or-rama."

The internet revolution was supposed to change the way we lived our lives. Most of that much trumpeted change hasn't hit us yet. But with more and more people having internet access at work and computers at home, some of the day to day stuff we do has changed. I check the news online, invest in stock through an online broker, book flights through a web site, and, most recently, purchased eighty pounds of discounted premium cat food for delivery straight to my home. (Okay, I was actually aiming for forty pounds, but I must have clicked that shopping cart twice. Damn my over-active finger…)

But what happens when the internet collides headlong with the queer community? The dot.com goes dot.gay, that's what.

There are queer web sites with news and entertainment features, like Gay.com and Planetout.com. And of course there are the gay and lesbian areas of good old America OnLine, the grand-mamma of the gay chat room, and many others like it.

Whether it's on AOL or any of the other services and sites offering chat, you can log on and dive right into your conversation of choice, whether it's dykes who dig powerful motorcycles (more vibration?) or men who just love the feel of real leather in their Jeeps. You can do friendly chat or sexy chat, depending on your need or preference.

And it doesn't matter whether you're in Paducah or Palm Springs. You've got mail.

One of the great things about the internet is that it is sort of a natural end to the problem of gay, lesbian, and bisexual isolation—the isolation many queer folks feel whether they're just coming out or they live in a small town. With the internet, you're never alone as a g/l/b person, because you can go to a gay site and connect with others like you. No more Saturday nights in Kalamazoo spent washing your hair—and trying to get as excited as the girl in the Herbal Essence commercial. No, siree!

Just imagine how much easier coming out would have been, if you could have just gone to a web site and found out about others like you—not just the images of Pride Parade out-takes on the evening news, where only the most outrageous need apply. Information is not recruitment, and accessible information can save lives. Just go to the net, kiddo.

And what would you pay for this fabulous ginsu knife set? But, wait, there's more!

Have you seen the ads? From "Romance at AOL" to M4M at Yahoo and Personals at Planetout.com, the days of dating options being limited to the guys you meet at bars or through the occasional rent-a-puppy trip to the park is over. We have on-line ads. Many of them come with photos. (Some more explicit than others, of course. Way more explicit.)

Just pick any city, and there are hundreds upon hundreds of ads. I like to look at them from sort of a voyeuristic perspective. I'm dating someone, but I have a friend who isn't. When I see an ad I like for him, I respond with his email address. (I'm a caring friend, after all. He'll thank me for it later. Really.) The one that really got me recently was the guy whose ad said, "I'm just looking for someone to put up the Christmas ornaments on the tree with." I'm a sap for a sweet line like that. Fortunately, so is my friend.

I actually know a gay couple who met through the net. They've been together for a year now. They got to know each other by email before they ever met, which took a lot of the "interview date" pressures off. They skipped right over the "should I talk with that guy at the bar with his friends who look like really angry bull dykes" moment. With the superficial stuff right out of the way, they moved on into a successful relationship.

But that's not all. If you're a couple looking for other couples as friends, post an ad! If you're a Barbie nut looking for other gay Barbie collectors, post an ad! If your gay dog needs a woof buddy, post an ad! If it's out there, it can come to you.

With the internet, the queer community keeps getting ever larger. And in the end, we all know that size matters. It's also getting more accessible to everyone, wherever they are. Thanks to the gay dot.coms, it's just a click away.

Who knew a finger could have this much fun?

PARTY OF FIVE

I'm waiting for the day I get to sleep with Rupert Everett. At least, I am prepared for the eventuality that someday I might get to sleep with Rupert Everett. One day. Somehow. Somewhere.

You just never know. And I'm prepared. Because he's in my party of five.

Party of five?

You see, my party of five is "the list." You know, the list of five celebrities that, if you had the opportunity ever—er, arise—to sleep with, you could, even if you're part of a couple, because he's on the list. I'm not sure where the idea originated, but I think it was an episode of *Friends*. It's sort of a game, and it's harmless fun. The idea is that there are five celebrities you can choose that you would like to sleep with, but if you did, it would- n't count as infidelity, because they were on the list.

So lots of my friends have their parties of five. Entries range from the obvious, like Tom Cruise, Brendan Frasier, Antonio Sabato, Jr., Ricky Martin, and Pierce Brosnan (though from the way Pierce dresses as Agent 007, you'd *think* he was a gay man), to the less obvious ones, like Chris O'Donnell or Jeremy Northram.

But I approach the list just a little differently. I insist that any celebrity on my list must pass one strict little test. He has to be openly gay. I mean, I may feel lust in my heart when I look at Brendan Frasier, but at the fore- front of my mind is, "Danger, Will Robinson! He's straight, so what's the point?" If I'm going to list my party of five, I want there to be at least the remote possibility (not just the, "Nicole, this is Tom calling—I'm really drunk, and Kev here is starting to look good to me"). Sure, there are a number of celebrities rumored to be gay, but they all come with a certain amount of baggage—namely, their wives.

Besides, I find that while I might lust after certain straight men in a theoretical sort of way, it's a very limited attraction, much the sort that I have toward women—an "oh, that's aesthetically pleasing, but what the hell would I do with it" response. (And I always love it that straight men think all gay men are attracted to them, when, because we know they're straight, of course we're not! Just as straight men generally seem to think that just because they're attracted to a beautiful lesbian, they somehow have more than a snowball's chance in hell of bedding her. But I digress. The straight male ego is generally a twisted wonder in and of itself, and many straight women have spent books attempting to understand it—unsuccessfully.)

In addition to the out-ness principle as applied to my list, there's another reason I only consider gay men, and it's a sizable difference. Did you catch the news of the Kinsey study a few months ago into the size of straight versus gay male penises? Yes, in a study published in of *Archives of Sexual Behavior*, noted sexologist Alfred Kinsey found that on average the penis sizes of gay men were longer and larger around than those of straight men. (I do my research, you see.)

So back to my list. My party of five is at this point only a party of four. There just aren't enough really cute, out gay celebrities to fill the fifth, though if Ricky Martin ever officially came out, he would be an automatic in. Fortunately, since I don't have the fifth now, that means any one of the four can count twice. And once is just never enough.

Number four on my list is Todd Oldham, the fashion designer. I've always had a thing for boy-next-door cute. Number three is George Michael, the only guy on the planet who actually makes topiary-trimmed facial hair look good. And he's not picky about locale, so his likelihood may actually be higher than one might think. Number two is Mitchell Andersen, one of the few truly out actors on American television. His movie *Relax, It's Just Sex* was a great preview of what he would be like. And of course, number one is dear old Rupert, a true leading man if ever there was one. He's played everything from gay best friend to king of the fairies—roles we're all more or less familiar with. If he could put aside the much-reported excess ego, he could definitely make an ideal husband.

So there it is. My gay party of five. Everyone should have one, just for the make-your-partner-a-little-bit-jealous factor, if nothing else.

And you never know. It could happen.

She's Got Legs

I've never shied away from tackling the major issues of the day. Gay marriage? I said, "Do it for the gifts." Gay adoption? So what if the kid's mom is named Bruce, as long as he's got two loving parents. Gays in the military? Don't ask me, and I won't tell you how angry I am over that episode in American absurdity. Gay fashion? Just say no to those damn white jeans. (Ticket to the clue bus to the un-informed: white makes your butt look LARGER. Unless, of course, that's the look you're going for.)

And then there are the really big issues of the day. Like chest hair. In a ground breaking column, I said, "Think trimmed, not shaved." Now, in the spirit of tackling yet another—er—hairy issue, I'm ready to take a new and important stand. Despite severe lobbying by Gillette, Remington, and even Epilady, I must announce that the ever increasing trend of gay men shaving their legs must be stopped, cut off, and washed down the drain like so much useless stubble.

You know what I'm talking about. If you go into any gay gym these days—and the inhabitants of gay gyms are often seen on the streets, in coffee houses, in clubs, and other public places—you'll notice that nearly every other buffed and wannabe buffed one among them has silky smooth legs. Leg shaving for men, which I thought was only a monstrous fad crossing over from the "serious" body builder set, has staked a big claim in the gay male community.

Now I know that the alleged rationale behind the leg shaving for men is that "it shows off the definition of your leg muscles." Unfortunately, it also makes those defined and muscled legs indistinguishable from the defined and muscled legs of Mary Lou Retton. And for the wannabe buffed set with skinnier legs, it makes them indistinguishable from the shapely legs of Mary Hart.

I have nothing against women shaving their legs if they want to, though I do think that they are more or less forced to do so by a male-dominated societal standard, as my best female friend is constantly reminding me. The principle is that women's legs are prettier and more pleasing to men if they're smooth. But why are gay men buying into that absurd of an idea? Part of what has distinguished men from women over at least the last 50 years is that men's legs are hairy, while women's are not. And even if my heart bleeds for the women who deal with shaving their legs day in and day out, the fact is that I have in my mind the perception that men's legs are hairy. Thus, I see shaved legs on a guy and think, "Wow. She's in guy drag."

With all the attention paid to gay men engaging in some sort of pursuit of hyper-masculinity at the gym, doesn't the leg shaving just make absolutely no sense whatsoever? The best argument to be made is that we are seeking our own standard of masculinity, and shaved legs may play a part in that standard. Unfortunately, I think it's more likely that everyone is just following a trend. Besides, the legs on a Ken doll are smooth and hard, and we all know what you find between HIS legs.

More importantly, I happen to like hairy legs on a guy, and I don't believe I'm alone in that. Yes, say it with me now, "Hairy legs are good. Mmmm. Mmmm. Good." The leg hair, especially if it's full enough to be noticeable, makes the legs look all the more masculine. There's not enough shape on most guys' legs—-unless the guy in question is Mr. Universe— to make there be enough of a difference in the view of their leg definition to justify the leg shaving.

In addition to the pure aesthetics of the matter, there are some very practical considerations. As with chest shaving, with leg shaving there is also that troublesome aspect of stubble. Ouch!! Having experienced face stubble burn on any number of mornings, I can only imagine the effects of leg stubble whip lash. "How'd you get that strangely shaped burn on your chest, Gus? And your cheek? And your arm? And…" It's just one more inconvenience in the way of physical intimacy. Besides, if I wanted a guy who could play music by rubbing the bristles on his legs together, I'd be dating a cricket.

So as a more or less responsible commentator on the mores of society and the generally pretty cool stuff around gay life, I must take my stand here. I will not allow the invasion of leg shaving to proceed unchecked. I will cry the battle cry, "Shave your face, not your legs!"

Gillette and Remington are gonna hate me.

GETTING WOOD AT THE TIMBERFELL

"Au naturel." The words just drip off your tongue like sweat off a shirtless circuit boy. Nude, as they say in the North. Nekkid, as they say in the South. And there are queer places where you can be exactly that.

Admit it, now. You've seen the ads at the back of the national gay magazines and the local publications. "A clothing optional resort for men." Or better, "Where clothing is NOT an option."

And you've wondered, "What's it like to stay at one of these places?" Is it like Sodom and Gomorrah on a stick? Or just a comfy retreat where you don't have to worry about accessorizing? Do you ever hear anyone say, "Hang on a minute. I'm getting dressed?" Do you dress up, right, or left for dinner? When you greet someone, do you shake hands? Is that all? When is it not polite to point?

Intrepid explorer that I am, I decided to seek some answers for my inquiring mind. I was ready to look real hard. To dig deep. To part the cheeks of darkness. To see the moon in a whole new light. To stop with the metaphors while I'm ahead.

But where would I go? What would I do? A resort on the coast? Too much like just another nude beach. A lake retreat? I'm not really into water sports. A Dude ranch? Aren't they all? Besides, there are too many cacti out West. Then I found the perfect option. A mountain hideaway! After all, I'm an earthy person. (Hey, I wore green on Earth Day.) This would be a true test of the clothing optional resort. I'd be going back to nature. Literally. Mountains, forest, and open sky—but would I be able to see the forest for the wood?

I made my reservation at the Timberfell Lodge in the Smoky Mountains. I had mental images of hiking through the woods in nothing but hiking books. Riding a horse bareback—just like on the greeting cards. Playing a game of croquet, with extra balls and mallets present.

We arrived to find a pleasant little lodge hidden away in insolated, mountainous terrain. We settled into our room, which was charming and rustic, and came with extra touches I liked. Instead of a mint on the pillow, there was a premium condom. The ceiling and the log headboard on the bed came equipped with eye-hooks, for those tie-me-up-tie-me-down moments, I suppose. Coincidentally, I had come to the lodge with Ben, a tall, handsome West Virginian who drives a pick-up truck, dances a mean two-step, and kisses like there's no tomorrow. Pointing to the hooks, I smiled sweetly and told him he would learn later what it meant to be subject to MY will. He just laughed. I guess he could tell I'm not really into M&M's…

I quickly learned a couple of things about clothing optional resorts. First, when it's 40 degrees outside, it's not really "optional," except at the jacuzzi area. My guess was that they named the place Timberfell after seeing a few nudist guests in cold weather. There would be no nude hiking for us. But the lodge was at the base of a mountain peak, which I HAD to climb, so we set out on the trail first thing. There was a lot of huffing and puffing on the way up, followed by gasps of satisfaction at the view. And we were fully clothed at the time.

The other thing I learned about clothing optional gay resorts is that folks who go there are really pleasant and fun. After a day of hiking or antiquing in the neighboring town, the guests, and their little dogs too, gathered in the lodge in front of the fire, to drink wine and snarf down appetizers. One big dinner later, we retired to the saloon, where Ben and I two-stepped, until the karaoke began.

I'd never done karaoke, since my Indian name is "Sings Like Cybill Shepherd," and neither had Ben. But we did a rendition of the Carpenters' "Close to You" with our arms around each other, our mouths close to a shared mike, and a dip-me-backward kiss to mark the end. It was probably vomitously cute, but no one tossed cookies.

When the singing finally died out, it was time for the jacuzzi—and trying not to freeze as we undressed to get in. But suffice it to say that no timber fell there. We sat in each other's arms, talking with the other couples soaking in the hot spray, until our skin became sufficiently prune-like to require a retreat. I told Ben that I knew what he would look like as an old man. He just pressed his wrinkled lips against mine.

We dried off, dressed, and walked hand in hand back to the lodge, under a clear sky lit by a full moon. The path glowed in the white light, clear and quiet, pristine and still. We fell asleep, some time later, waking in the morning to the smell of coffee and the sound of hiking boots on hardwood floors.

It wasn't quite the naturist expedition I had expected. More exposure—in warmer weather—might be even more fun. But would I go back?

Naturally.

Couples Waltz.
A Mostly Up-beat Dance With Frequent
Turns and Occasional Dips

Jumping the Broom

I went to the Big Gay Wedding of the century this weekend. I was warned by my date that this was no ordinary affair. The couple in question included a church organist and a wedding planner. I knew I should be afraid. Very afraid.

That was before I learned that there was a pre-ceremony concert at the church at three, followed by the two-hour wedding service at four, promptly on the chiming of the hour. By now I was shaken. But I was stirred, so I went with some anticipation.

What the two grooms couldn't get in legality, they made up for in pomp and circumstance. The wedding program was 23 pages long. There were 14 attendants. A full church choir. A 14-piece orchestra. Several organists and pianists. A dozen vocal soloists. Two ministers. A photographer AND a videographer. And an official wedding coordinator fluttering about.

It was the Mother of All Weddings.

The flowers, though tastefully done, included all the colors of the rainbow flag—lest we forget it was a gay wedding, I suppose. Even the corsages on the mothers (there was a set of honorary parents to go with the real ones) had the same sextet of colors, and the men's boutonnieres were exquisite miniatures of the corsages. When a gay couple goes over the top, they do it in style.

The happy couple incorporated every tradition you could possibly think of into their wedding. From attendants to rings to taking communion and exchanging vows. The only tradition they didn't fit in was the throwing of a bouquet, as I noted to one of the groomsmen. ("How will the next person know they're gonna get married?" I complained.)

But my favorite tradition that they observed was one I hadn't seen before. As the African American minister explained, during the time of slavery in this country—which wasn't really so very long ago—marriages between African American slaves weren't recognized. (Sound like anything in current society?) So in order to memorialize their relationship, a couple would jump over a broom, signifying their entry into a new life together—much like stepping over a threshold in other traditions. Our newlywedded grooms jumped with surprising grace over a not-surprisingly elegant broom, to the applause of the entire church. And then they were off down the aisle together.

Though my rear end was not happy after three hours on a wooden pew, the reception more than made up for the hard time spent. It was held in a restored Craftsman-style hall adjacent to a park. There were mounds of flowers in rainbow colors, lavish buffets, flowing wine, and (without meaning to be a size queen) the biggest wedding cake I've ever seen. It topped out at over five feet tall. With spires.

Yes, foregoing the traditional tackiness of two grooms holding hands (which, admittedly, I've always thought were cute anyway), they had somehow managed to make the cake look like a Gothic cathedral. They must have been curious why I peered into the windows—I was wondering if I would see people inside.

I also couldn't help but wonder, as the Democrats and Republicans do battle in Washington, if many of their number are thinking about how a whole segment of society doesn't have a legal right that everyone else takes for granted? That, as in the time of slavery, we gay folks mostly create our own rituals to formalize our relationships. Our own jumping of the broom. And that so far only Vermont has started down the right path in recognizing our life partnerships, the way legal marriage recognizes straight ones and—in the not-too-distant past—once just recognized white ones.

After I'd recovered from my initial shock at the size of the cake, I smiled as the brother of one of the grooms toasted the couple. "I hope you know what you're getting into with MY brother," he laughed to his new brother-in-union. Then the newlyweds fed each other cake (miraculously, without toppling a single spire), and they moved to the dance floor for the traditional first waltz.

I left the wedding after dancing with the rest of the guests to the traditional rendition of the Village People's "Y.M.C.A." But as I walked through the door, I heard my name called out. I turned just in time to catch a small table bouquet that a groomsman threw my way.

I hope that someday—even if less lavishly in style—that maybe, just maybe, I'll be jumping the broom, too.

THE VALENTINE'S DAY CURSE

The pressure is on. I like a little bit of pressure now and then, but I like it to involve candles, massage oil, and Sven, the hunky Swedish massage therapist. Unfortunately, the pressure I'm talking about is the countdown pressure for Valentine's Day.

You see, Valentine's Day is a lot like sex. Both bring horrific new meaning to the term "performance anxiety." Both can be really great—or really awful—but in either case you can be sure you're being graded by your partner. It's part of the Valentine's Day curse.

As I began to ponder the upcoming cursed day, I began to wonder. Is it just coincidence that the initials for Valentine's Day—V.D.—are the same as the initials for some seriously unpleasant illnesses? Illnesses involving pain, discomfort, and insanity? After all, Valentine's Day can be about as much fun as a case of the (fill in your least favorite disease here)—always for the single, and especially for the coupled.

The trick to minimizing the Valentine's Day curse is to plan ahead. Carefully. Particularly if you happen to be part of a couple.

We've all done the big heart-shaped box of chocolates thing. I call this the basic "Forrest Gump" approach to the Valentine's Day gift. You're basically hoping a gooey center will get you to a gooey center.

Roses are almost always required, but roses alone are never enough to carry the whole day. Nope, there's got to be something suitably special. Edible underwear? Sticky—not necessarily in a good way—and way too 1980's Traci Lord. But it might win you some retro points.

Maybe a certificate to a day spa for the two of you is the way to go. Most day spas do couples activities now, where you lie beside each other on tables having all sorts of luxurious things done to you. Massage, facials—you name it. For my money, nothing says romance like a couple getting their butts waxed together.

I've always liked the idea of showing up to greet your Valentine in an overcoat and a jock strap. (Cup optional.) For the women, the Xena, Warrior Princess outfit is a particularly effective alternative to the aforementioned athletic supporter. (Though an unusually androgynous lesbian pal of mine used to enjoy wearing a cup for the shock value.) In any case, surprise always wins you the extra bonus round, as long as the surprise is a good one. (No "Buns of Steel" videotapes or Richard Simmons "Slimmons" candy, please!)

If you know of any fun bed and breakfast inns close by, you could surprise your partner with a quick weekend getaway. Take some soft music and candles. Or if your mate has a good sense of humor, rent yourself a room at the sleaziest motel in town, preferably one that rents by the hour. Bring hot oil and costumes.

And what about the single among us? That jock strap under the overcoat thing can work really well for GETTING you the Valentine you've been hankering after. Just make sure his boyfriend isn't home when you show up, and that you're not violating any restraining orders that you're aware of. (Stalking is only funny if you're a kitten and he's a toy mouse.) And be sure to check that there haven't been any reports of flashers in the area first. Valentine's Day evening at the police station is NOT a fun option, unless you're really into the jailhouse scene.

Of course, being single at Valentine's has its advantages. None of the Valentine's Day gift planning pressure applies to you. You can kick back, relax and gloat that you don't have to run around looking for the "right" gift like all of your coupled off friends. Heck, you can even have a little fun at their expense. Just send yourself some fabulous roses at the office/at the coffee shop where you hang out/at your favorite queer bar, and watch all the couples squirm. Nobody likes to be out-Valentined, and you raised the bar for all of them.

Besides, on Valentine's Day evening, you are statistically more likely to get laid than any other night of the year besides New Year's Eve. (That's my story and I'm sticking to it.) So go out, reach out, and touch someone. Just don't try a line like, "Hi, I'm Cupid. Wanna see the size of my arrow?"

MAPLE SYRUP AND MATZO BALLS

I'm seriously considering becoming a Reform Jew in Vermont.

Yes, this new millennium's barely off the ground, and I'm liking it better than the last one already. The Reform Jews have declared that gay relationships are "worthy of affirmation" through Jewish same-sex union ceremonies. Yes, that's right. We're goin' to the synagogue, and we're gonna get maa-aa-aa-ried. So here we have a major religious group that has unequivocally announced (none of that gentile waffling on the issue here) that gay unions deserve blessing. I think I want to convert. I'll be like a gay Sammy Davis, Junior. Sort of. Thank God I'm already circumcised.

Just think of the great ceremonies we'll have! Jewish weddings are always a blast, so I can only imagine how much fun a Jewish union with a little queer magic will be. And from a practical perspective, not only is a yarmulke (for the gentiles among us, that's the small cap worn on the crown of the head) a sign of respect for God, but it has the added benefit of covering up your partner's bald spot. Poof! No more unsightly head shine. This could really cut into the gay Rogaine market, but it seems to me that finding your spouse even more attractive probably leads to a more fulfilling and lasting union, right? Why not give it a head start, so to speak? (Note: if you're a Patrick Stewart type, forget about the head shine thing and just engage, baby, engage!)

Not long after the Reform Jewish rabbis announced their vote, the state of Vermont produced something even more impressive than Ben & Jerry's ice cream. With some powerful prodding by the Vermont courts, the legislature passed—and the governor signed into law—a "civil unions" law, which gives gay and lesbian couples all of the state rights available to married couples. Yes, we can go to Vermont and get our committed relationships recognized by the state. I'd say this is the most significant development in the struggle for gay equality in—well—the entire millennium.

That giant sucking sound you hear is the sound of queers all over the country packing up their wardrobes, their power tools, and their family pets to move up to Vermont. My own thinking is that living in a state where you can actually marry your partner could be a big quality of life issue for a lot of people. I guess this means I'll have to relocate soon, too. I suppose I could learn to like Birkenstocks. And while I'm not fond of icy weather, I do love snow. Besides, I've always enjoyed maple syrup. In many, many ways.

Speaking of syrup, George W. Bush met with gay Republicans recently and sweetly confirmed to his surprise that they are indeed human. Of course, he didn't meet with those pesky Log Cabin Republicans (there's the syrup again), who had the nerve to endorse John McCain (who met with them, minus the syrup) in the primary. Despite the meeting, Bush still opposes non-discrimination laws protecting gays in the workplace and gay marriage (note to GW: don't go to Vermont).

But Bush said he was "a better person" for meeting with the carefully selected group of gay and lesbian Republicans. He also said he is "mindful that we're all God's children" (note to GW again: the Reform Jews have already figured this out). Though it is unclear what effect, if any, the meeting will have on the Republican stance on gay rights, it was at least a baby step in the right direction. Which brings me right back to syrup again, because we all know that syrup moves really, really slowly.

When George "Dubya" Bush is talking to gay folks, Reform Jews are blessing gay unions, and those scrappy Vermonters are making the gay civil unions legal, I'd say things are headed firmly in the right direction.

I can't wait to move to Vermont. There's a yarmulke there with my name on it.

THIS OLD GAY HOUSE

Move over, Bob Vila. Hasta la vista, HGTV. Take a hike back to K-Mart, Christopher Lowell. Welcome to the first episode of This Old Gay House.

Yes, today's show is dedicated to those tireless queer couple fixer-uppers—the ones who transform old, tired, run-down houses into hip, trendy, immaculately restored personal castles. You know, the ones with rainbow flags on the front steps and the kick-ass crown molding plainly visible in the foyer.

Until recently, when a sudden break-up intervened, I was planning to join the hordes of happy homo homeowners busily learning how to use caulk guns and tile grout. Even if my own entry into their illustrious number may have been delayed (I admit, I am a coward around a tool kit, and I just didn't want to do it alone—some things are a lot less fun solo), I thought I should at least prepare myself for the experience.

After all, though I may be a little biased, there seem to be more re-modelers per capita in the gay world than in the straight. And often, these old houses are the sometimes loving, sometimes acrimonious projects of long-term gay and lesbian couples. So I decided to talk with one of these couples, especially for today's show.

Keith and Doug are a particularly experienced couple of home boys. Partnered for seven years, they are in their second house together—both of which they have remodeled. Keith is a bit on the professorial but slightly manic side, while Doug is a laid-back engineer type who knows how to put hardwood in. In other words, they are well matched. But more importantly for today's show, you could say they've been around the block a few times—from the fixer upper house perspective, that is. (While some of us may have been around the block with fixer upper boyfriends. Hint: You have a better chance of fixing up a house.)

And in speaking with Keith and Doug, I learned a few useful rules about home renovations for the homo-alone couple. (That last pun hurt me as much as it hurt you.)

Rule Number One. Cover up well when painting. Backing into wet pain while naked (particularly if you're a hairy guy) is not as much fun as those Farah Fawcett nude body-painting videos would lead you to believe. But nothing says I love you like spending a Saturday evening stripping paint from your partner's backside. And if you let it dry, you get the added bonus of saving money on a body waxing. Pull and play!

Rule Number Two. Buy your partner tools (and other related presents). Says Keith, "I bought Doug a leather tool belt for his birthday." And did he wear it? I asked. "First he wore it without the tools—or anything else," Keith replied. Hmmm, I thought, this puts kitchen remodeling in a whole new light, doesn't it?

Rule Number Three is perhaps the most important one: Decide who's in charge. It doesn't always have to be the same person, but as in the bedroom, it helps to have somebody lead the way—even if there is the occasional tongue-lashing involved (take that as you wish). As Doug explains, "You have to figure out who's really in charge, but you let the other person think that he is. I like to let Keith think he's in charge, but ultimately somebody's got to make the final decision, and that would be me." Adds Keith, "Usually, there's some level of screaming, but there's consensus at the end." Again, not unlike sex.

Rule Number Four. Try to realize where relationship issues are coming in—and ignore them. Keith and Doug's worst remodeling experience happened in their first house. They couldn't agree on room colors, so their compromise was to divvy up the rooms between them. This was a bad idea. Between Keith's muted tastes and Doug's bold color choices, it looked like Martha Stewart had just had a knock-down-drag-out with

Andy Warhol. So they learned to separate their desires for personal identities from the painting of their rooms. They grew as a couple and as remodelers.

Rule Number Five. A little renovation is never enough. "Keith started with the bathroom wallpaper," Doug says with a grin. "Then he wanted to replace the moldings, then the fixtures, and then re-tile the floor. Changing wallpaper became a complete bathroom renovation." In other words, the wallpaper was just foreplay? Doug smiled and responded, "You gotta think big." I liked the sound of *that*.

On that note, we've reached the end of today's show. Tune in next time, when we'll be walking through a work-in-progress bungalow with a single lesbian owner, asking the important questions: Is it really as much fun solo? Can better tools replace a partner?

Until then, this is Kevin Isom, for This Old Gay House, saluting all the gay and lesbian HOMOwners out there painting and scraping and hammering away. We like the sound of *that!*

Last Tango.
When Your Dance Partnership Has
Exceeded its Sell-By Date

You've Lost That Luvin' Feelin'?

Lust may not last, but sex drives are forever. Just ask Bill Clinton.

So what happens when you've been in a relationship for a while, and slowly you notice—can we talk?—that you're buying condoms, lubricant and other assorted accoutrements way less often than you used to do. In fact, there's dust on the packaging, and you vaguely recall that near the beginning of your relationship you got frequent flyer miles for all your purchases at the local drug store or gay-friendly supply shop.

Then the realization hits: Bob Dole is having more sex than you are. And you don't even need Viagra.

It's a condition commonly known among women as lesbian bed-death. Among men, it's non-penis-envy.

Maybe you're thinking, "I got together with a man, not a boy. Especially not the Pillsbury Dough Boy!" Maybe he's thinking, "Hey, I married Mr. Atlas. Who is this skinny little roadmap?" Maybe you're both thinking, "Tell me again—why did I let this woman show up with a U-Haul?"

Perhaps you find yourself enjoying eyeing the guys at the gym just a little too often, a little too long. Perhaps he's decided to take dance lessons at one of the local gay clubs—and doesn't want you to come along. So while your partner's at his dance class and you're at the gym, you ask a guy you've met if he's had dinner yet. He hasn't, and after your work out, you go out. You can tell he likes you, and he finds you charming, a feeling you've forgotten you used to feel. You talk about the foibles of dating, like how you would only go out with a guy if he called within 24 hours of getting your phone number, and you begin to bond. At the end of dinner, he says, "I guess I'd better call you tomorrow, so I can make your 24 hour rule." You smile, and it feels good.

Now maybe you realize that you've got yourself a wee bit of a problem.

You could consult the experts. Like the author of *Husband Hunting Made Easy*, Patrick Price. In *Husband Hunting*, Price suggests that problems in the sexual arena in otherwise good relationships generally come from two sources: insecurity and boredom. (Though, of course, if the relationship itself isn't working, you've got a whole other set of issues. In that case, the no-sex scenario is just another step on the road to Divorce Court.)

If boredom is the cause, then the time apart, including dance lessons and dinner with a new friend, is a good thing—an expression or reassertion of independence. You're combating the boredom, tickling your inner child, man-handling your manhood. (But if the dancing is an excuse to get out of the prison that is your relationship, and the dinner with a new friend is a cry for romance, then you're either really, really bored or back on that aforementioned road to Divorce Court.)

If, on the other hand, insecurity is the cause, try telling your partner that he's looking mighty tasty tonight. Or tell your girlfriend that you'd like to see her coming toward you in black lace and stiletto heels—carrying a whip.

In any case, don't forget to jazz things up. You might try turning off all the lights at night, opening all the blinds, and taking your partner on the living room floor. The open blinds add just the right hint of danger of exposure to spice things up, while the cover of night really does shield you from prying neighborly eyes. (Note: This does not work in a ground floor apartment.) Houses with secluded, low-level (think fear of heights) balconies are good for this purpose, too. Bend over the railing, baby!

Along similar lines, a visit to a novelty shop wouldn't be a bad idea, either. A couple who buys toys together stays together. Or at least gets a lot of laughs. You'll ask each other questions like, "Honey, does this look realistic—or even physically possible—to you?" As a general rule, if the answer is "Hell, no!" then you've found a fun new toy.

If the relationship is a good one worth preserving, you've got to be willing to work on the sex part. That's right, work. Think of sex as an occupation with perks. It's a dirty job, but somebody's got to do it.

With a little luck and perseverance, you might well find that you haven't lost that luvin' feelin' at all. You only misplaced it for a while.

Still Miss You, Baby, But My Aim's Gettin' Better

I looked up an old flame in the phone book the other day. He wasn't there. I called information. He wasn't listed, either published or non. I inquired around. He'd moved.

And I hadn't noticed.

I say that with some surprise, because I recall it wasn't all that long ago that I was really smitten with this man. I'd picked out the china and booked the chapel, too. I had thrown out my Gloria Gaynor and become fond of Gloria Estefan instead.

And when he and I had broken up, because of some unresolved feelings he had about his ex—a condition I like to refer to as "nostalgia"—I'd had a seriously bad case of the achy brakey heart. The inconsolable, play a show tune, get-vaguely-suicidal-or-homicidal-depending-on-the-tune sort of heartbreak. It was a bleak time, and one that I made my steadfast friends suffer through with me. Yes, I was Scarlet without her Mammy, devastated over losing Ashley far, far away from Tara. Okay, so I was a little melodramatic, too.

After all, it wasn't that long before that everyone we knew had commented how cute we were together, what a perfect couple we seemed to make, and all the other malarkey that people tell a couple who aren't throwing small appliances at each other. Of course, it was true that we were awfully cuddly-happy-smiley, both in public and in private. We made Siamese twins look cold and distant.

Until his case of nostalgia hit, like a dark storm breaking wind across an unsuspecting land. Like Aunt Mary coming to visit your roommate the bull dyke when there's no Midol in the house. Like a vegetarian with hemorrhoids at a sit-down barbecue.

I began the process of recovery—a continuing status I like to refer to as "re-treading"—and moving on with my life. But relationships that end badly—and how often is a non-mutual break up ever good?—usually leave the breaker feeling free but slightly guilty, while the breakee feels hurt. And then later, betrayed. And then later still, really, really ticked off. It's a natural progression of feelings. For confirmation, you need look no further than one of our greatest sources of wisdom on the subject, country music. "I Still Miss You, Baby, But My Aim's Getting' Better." "I Feel So Bad, It's Like You're Still Here." Or my personal favorite, "My Baby Ran Off With My Best Friend, And I Sure Miss Him [My Friend]." You think I'm making these up, don't you? Think again.

In my own achy brakey case, after the initial hurt, I'd gone though the angry phase. I battled my desires to put him on the Church of Latter Day Saints video mailing list. I fought my impulse to call the Rogaine one-eight-hundred telephone number on his behalf. I resisted any urge to get him a free trial membership in the International Corporal Punishment Club. (Not that I necessarily succeeded, but I tried.)

I got on with my life, until that surprising day when I discovered that he had moved out of town, and I hadn't even known it. Which was a day, in its surprise, that almost made up for the pain of the relationship's nostalgic demise. Because while it's true that revenge is sweet, it's even sweeter when you don't want it anymore, and you know you're completely over those feelings of heartbreak. The day when you wake up and think, "Oh, whatever. It doesn't matter any more" is one of the best days of your life.

It's a watershed moment. Like the day you found out Greg Louganis was gay. Or that an openly gay or lesbian candidate had won a public office. Or that your landlord had decided not to raise the rent this year. Or you played a country song backward, and you got your dog back, your house back, your truck back…A day you wanted to stand up and cheer.

You suddenly realize about your ex, "He was such an indecisive person. I'm really glad he was able to actually reach a decision to leave. We're both better for it. It left me free to find someone better for me."

So Cute-Guy-Formerly-Known-As-Boyfriend, if you're out there and you think this song is about you, you're only partly right. Because, you see, it's true.

I still miss you, baby, but my aim's gettin' better.

SEPARATION ANXIETY

"Honey, I think that we should separate."

Four years and two cats into our relationship, the words fell like cold water on a hot stove. Like the executioner's blade on Anne Boleyn. Like the most painful, devastating thing I could imagine. Yet oddly, at that moment, the thing I was thinking was, "We just went to Sam's Wholesale Club together two days ago. Who buys in BULK two days before announcing a separation?" Was he really concerned that we'd run out of toilet paper and laundry detergent?

But then, my thought patterns are like that. Even in the midst of searing pain, I tend to see the lighter side. For this character trait, I blame my dad, a man for whom a happy pill would be redundant—I often carry a buffalo-strength tranquilizer dart gun when I visit him. Dad used to like to liven up funerals, for heaven's sake. I'd be paying my respects to the deceased person lying in state, when suddenly I'd hear. "Psst! Could you scratch my nose? I've got an itch, and I'm just a little stiff today!" And there I would be, laughing hysterically over the deceased, as some poor family looked on in horror. True, I became adept at making laughter look like weeping, but I never mastered throwing my voice the way Dad did.

In the ensuing days since my life change (gotta love euphemisms) occurred, I've re-learned some of the great things about being a gay person. The most important among them has been remembering the value of the strong friendships that we form. Like my gay and lesbian friends who said to me, "Get out now. Don't wait. He's made a decision—let him live with it. Don't prolong your own pain."

93

And they did more than that. They helped me to move to my new place just a couple days later. (I am efficient when motivated, despite anything my editor may tell you to the contrary, and I found a fabulous apartment the very next day after "the talk.") In fact, during the move my friends did most of the heavy lifting, knowing that I really wasn't in a mental state to calculate get-the-sofa-through-the-door spatial dynamics. Who knew that muscles actually did something other than filling out a tight t-shirt? Or that one lesbian and a tool belt can single-handedly re-wire a cable connection?

Then they stayed with me every night for a week. Not all at once, mind you. That would have looked too much like a pajama party, and I am not an Annette Funicello queen—I never got the whole Frankie Avalon thing. But my friends stayed with me, because it's tough to sleep alone, in a new place, when you keep rolling over looking for HIM—except that HE'S chosen not to be there any more. Not to belabor Annette, but it's no fun being on a beach blanket alone when the party's moved on. So I coped with it the same way she would have—I called in the Mouseketeers! The gay ones, that is.

I've noticed, as time has passed, that I've become very demanding on my friends in terms of physical reassurance. I need lots of affection. No less than five hugs a day. "Hug me now," I announce. Pause. Tap foot. "No, not in a minute. Now. You WILL comply." My Trekkie friends have taken to calling me "Seven of Need." (If you've never watched Star Trek: Voyager, you didn't get that.) It's part of the healing process.

At this point, whether this separation is truly only that—or turns out to be a divorce—is unclear. A lot depends on things like couples counseling and working through personal issues. And on whether love can survive all that. Heaven knows the Kleenex will. I have that in bulk.

But one thing is clear. With these queer friends of mine, I will survive.

Author's Note: It WAS a divorce, and I survived. Move over, Gloria Gaynor!

Breakin' Up Is Hard to Do

Did you ever wonder, when you were growing up, why there were so many, many songs on the radio about how hard breaking up can be? Did you think, "These adults have got to be exaggerating this stuff. Probably because they don't want us kids dating too soon."

Then you get a little older, you realize you're queer, and you think, "Oh, those songs are all by straight folks about straight people. I'm gay. It'll be totally different."

And then you go through a serious break up or two, and you realize, "Oh, wait. One size really DOES fit all."

As I've gotten older, each time a relationship hasn't worked out, I think, "Well, if this ever happens again, it can't possibly feel this bad." Sort of like an immunization shot. Next time you get that break up flu bug, it'll roll right off you. ("We're breaking up? Why, I'll just take some Vitamin C!") But it's never quite that simple.

Welcome to the real world. And no, I don't mean some fabulous apartment in an exotic setting where MTV has put you up with some total strangers and a camera crew. I mean the gee-this-is-no-fun, why-did-I-choose-this-guy-when-I-could-have-had-a-V-8 world of break ups and move outs.

Sometimes it's all about bad timing. Maybe you weren't really ready for a serious relationship when he was, and by the time you're ready for a lasting commitment in your life, he isn't really sure any more. Or worse, maybe he says the classic lines, "I don't know who I am any more. I need to find myself."

Trust me. Poking him in the ribs and saying, "I know who you are. You're [Fill in His Name Here]. There you go! You're found! Problem solved!" most definitely does not work. But it's worth a try, for the make-him-squirm factor if nothing else.

Even though you're pretty well prepared for the icky stuff you're going to have to go through (having listened to all those songs on the radio), there are still some little things that you're never quite prepared for.

Like, there's always a last time the two of you have sex. But you never know it at the time. You look back later, and you think, "Oh. That was the last time. I wish I'd known. I would have loved him better." Or at least you would have broken out the flamenco band and the Siamese twin jugglers, to give the moment a special send off.

And then there are the children. His dog has adopted you as dad, and your cat has done the same with him. You know you'll miss the animal, and she'll miss you. You worry about your own animal missing him. Even worse, you know they'll miss each other: your cat's been licking his dog's butt. And lately she looks like she's starting to enjoy it.

So you try to cope. You think, "There has to be something good out of all this." And having grown up hearing that annoying piece of parental advice, "Think of it as a learning experience," you wonder what lessons you've learned for next time, if and when you ever consider entering into another relationship.

Things like, learn to build lower walls around yourself, not higher ones—you want to lower the obstacles in your next relationship, not raise them. And realize that people change over time, so don't assume he won't, and try not to let it catch you by surprise if he does. Or learn to love him every moment as if it were your last—just not, of course, in a "Fatal Attraction" sort of way.

It's actually rather funny, this whole break up thing. What other situation lets you experience every emotion you've ever felt in your entire life all in one not-so-tidy package? ("Welcome to the show, Pandora. This is your life!")

But it is survivable. Even thrive-able, after time does its work, along with aromatherapy, massages, stress-relieving work-outs, a fun vacation or two, and possibly a good psychotherapist.

And before too long, you'll be ready to—pardon me—to put your tongue in someone else's cheek.

SANTA, BABY

'Tis the season! Yes, this is my annual opportunity to sit on a fat man's lap and tell him my secrets! So, Santa, Baby, if it's not too late, open up your arms and prepare your lap for my landing. And I'll try not to wiggle too much—after all, I remember what happened the last time.

Now, not to push you out of the closet, Santa, but can you explain to me why you live alone at the North Pole with a bunch of male elves? Is Mrs. Claus really a fag hag? Or a drag elf? What's the real story behind Rudolph's red nose? Just what kind of reindeer games is he into? Did you choose the North Pole because it had a really nice ring to it? And is "ho, ho, ho" truly a laugh, or did you sleep with a Circuit Party guy whose name you can't recall?

But wait, I'm supposed to be asking you for things. You can just keep your personal secrets in your sling—er, sleigh.

As I sit here thinking on it, I honestly don't need any material things this year, Santa, though if you have a French chateau with a white picket fence in your bag, you won't hear me objecting. And with respect to the question, "Who wants to be a millionaire?"—do I really need to answer that?

So the things that I want may be harder for you to put your fingers on.

I'd like a few more states to follow Vermont's example and give us civil union or marriage laws. I mean, I do love taffy and syrup, but I'm really not keen on moving into a snowy state just so I can get legally hitched. My basic rule is simple: sticky is fun, frozen is not.

I've really enjoyed seeing so many more gay folks on TV this year (though I think maybe the lives of the characters on Showtime's *Queer as Folk* don't really resemble anything like the life I lead). But what I'd really like is to be able to see queer folks playing themselves in real life a lot more comfortably.

I'd like to be able to walk down a beach with my partner holding hands and not get stared at—or glared at—by strangers. I'd like for a date to feel comfortable leaning across a table in any restaurant to give me a quick peck on the lips. After all, I'm an affectionate kind of guy, as you can tell from having me on your lap, and I'm a little tired of feeling always conscious of who is where and when around me. It's a little like living your life under siege—and intentionally ignoring the feeling.

Next, Santa, I thought I'd throw out a few tougher requests. I'd like for compassionate conservatism to mean something good. I'd like for George W. Bush to embrace the gay citizens that he now, against many of our wills, represents. I want Dick Cheney to talk openly and proudly of his lesbian daughter. And I want Jerry Falwell to support Tinky Winky's lifestyle.

I'd like for Will of TV's *Will & Grace* to get himself a nice boyfriend. At least for more than one episode. His spinsterhood is starting to remind me of my great-aunt Agnes. It's depressing me, Santa. He's cute, he's smart, and he can't seem to snag a lousy two-episode boyfriend?

I'd like to learn answers to my questions about dating. Like, why is it that any man willing to describe himself as "a great catch"—usually isn't? Or that any guy who thinks of himself as "caring and giving" is really a black hole of selfishness and need who'll suck you down quicker than Johnny Walker Red down a young George W. Bush?

As for me, Santa, 2000 was eventful in my life. I came out with my first book. I finished a novel. I started on *It Only Hurts When I Polka*. And I lost the person who was most important to me.

As I like to tell it, midway through the year, I discovered that my four and a half year relationship had exceeded its sell-by date. And that I'm currently looking for a boyfriend in the non-perishable goods section. In retrospect, Santa, I probably should have left him a year before. But I held on as long as I possibly could. Because I wanted to believe in something lasting.

I still do.

That's why I still believe in you. So if you've got those wishes down, Santa, there's no need to call security—I'll climb down off your lap now. I'll see you at the same time, same place, same season, next year.

Maybe by then I'll have that life partner thing all ironed out. And if I don't, then you can talk to me about one of those hot little single elves.

Queer as Polka.
Sometimes It's Just Plain Odd

Bank on It!

Sometimes you can see a bad idea coming. Like the time I got hot, heavy, and quite naked with my then-boyfriend in my cushy chair. The one on casters. On the hardwood floor. In the bedroom with the door that didn't latch well. And opened outward. Onto the hallway leading to the living room, where my roommate and his guests were visiting.

With legs slung over the padded arms of the chair, the motion of the ocean started the chair to rolling. Right to the door that opened wide, sending us sailing down the hall and across the living room, in corpus delicti, wearing nothing but really surprised expressions on our faces. Which, of course, paled in comparison to the surprise of my roommate and his friends.

To his credit, my roommate sprang to his feet, turned the chair about, and rolled us right back into the bedroom. Which was might nice of him as separation at that moment would have been a wee bit on the tricky side. "This is what I get for living with a blond," he told his guests breezily.

To this day, I still have that chair, but I only keep it in a carpeted room. I learned. Casters and hardwood—bad idea.

But sometimes you hear about an idea that makes you stop and think, "Wow. Why didn't anybody think of this before?" (How was that for a segue way?)

The good idea I have in mind involves semen, too, though it doesn't involve sex. Or chairs on casters. Instead, it involves what, with male and female sex, could be the result of the chair on casters experience. I'm talking about reproduction. Sperm and egg. Yin and yang. Children.

You see, there's a California sperm bank that has a different focus than most. It's like a bank that prefers gay money, only it prefers gay deposits of another kind. (Just avoid the drive-through teller window. Trust me.)

Based in Oakland, the Rainbow Flag Health Services (their web site is www.gayspermbank.com—catchy, isn't it?) is offering to provide a means for gay men and lesbians who want biological children to reproduce— without the child having the stigma of a daddy known only as "donor." In fact, Rainbow Flag's policy is simple. Gay sperm donors are actively recruited ("Be all that you can be! Like, a dad!"), the number of recipients of a donor's sperm is very limited (the opposite of the concept seemingly employed by straight male athletes and rock stars), the child-bearing mom is told the identity of the donor, and she agrees to make contact with him after the child is born.

The advantages are obvious. First, lesbians are often more comfortable dealing with gay men than they are with straight men, and this gives the mothers an option of having a father in the child's life without having to deal with prejudice and bigotry. That, and the gay man can decorate the child's room AND teach him how to have a body all the girls will drool over. In any case, the mothers and child are connected to the gay male community. And that can't be a bad thing.

Another advantage that Rainbow Flag touts is that since the donor may have fathered up to three other children, and those children and their lesbian mothers will be connected by the father (okay, this part does sound a little on the 1800's Mormon side), the child will have half-siblings in lesbian households nearby. And, as Rainbow Flag points out, since each child will know who his or her siblings are, they won't accidentally start dating in high school. (Let that sink in for a moment. You know that that was WAY too odd for me to have made up.)

Finally, Rainbow Flag notes that unlike with other sperm banks, the child will grow up knowing that not only did daddy want to help the mommies have a child, daddy cared enough to want to be a part of the child's life. Other sperm banks recruit donors through money. I can only imagine what kind of guys think, "Gee, I could use some extra cash today. Why don't I go play with myself into a plastic cup?" (Can we say, "Eee-eeuuw!"?)

All in all, Rainbow Flag seems to offer a good solution to lesbian families who want children, and to gay men who want to be fathers but can't adopt or make arrangements with a surrogate mother themselves.

After all, parenting is about wanting to raise a child, and Rainbow Flag creates a means for gay folks to do just that. And is that a good idea?

I'd bank on it.

FRENCH TICKLER

I'm always just a bit afraid when I sit down to write that I'll feel a little like Elizabeth Taylor's fifth husband. I'll know what to do, but I won't know how to make it interesting.

Fortunately, there's always something in this gay old world of ours that merits a giggle or two. So how about focusing on two of my favorite things in the news lately? Like lesbians and the French.

Sure, lesbians and the French might seem like an odd combination. Until you realize how much they have in common. They both know they could rule the world if they wanted to, but they're way too cool for that. Their talents run the gamut from exceptional cooking to powerful muscle. (The French show theirs by exploding nuclear weapons in deep ocean tests. Thankfully, the lesbians mainly stick to lifting heavy things.) With the French, love 'em or hate 'em, you gotta get tickled by 'em. And the French, it seems, have a thing for American lesbians. Ooh, la, la, baby!

It reached a let-them-eat-cake peak not so long ago with an article in the French magazine *Marie-Claire*. "For us," began the piece, "female homosexuality remains discreet, even clandestine. On the other side of the Atlantic, lesbians are quite visible. Like in Atlanta, where they have created their own city, their schools, their clinics, their churches." Most of which they built themselves, the magazine did not add. (Okay, I'm just kidding about the building it themselves part.)

The story included a short glossary of terms for the un-informed—words like "dyke," "butch," "fem," "lipstick lesbian," and "turkey baster." (You think I'm kidding about the turkey baster part, but I'm not.) The writer viewed the lesbian community with mixed emotions, describing a lesbian commitment ceremony as a "hallucination," at the same time that she questioned the wisdom of the women's creation of their own lesbian "ghetto."

Next a Paris TV producer flew to Atlanta to film footage for a segment of a French TV show roughly equivalent to *Sixty Minutes*. She went to Decatur, perhaps best described as one of the sub-cities within the larger metro Atlanta, where she interviewed the Digging Dykes of Decatur, a lesbian gardening group beloved at the annual Pride Parade for their Playskool lawn mowers and big straw flowered hats.

She said she hopes her TV segment will encourage gay viewers in France to be more open about their sexual orientation and thus create a more visible gay presence in France. Which, after what Catherine Deneuve did for the image of French lesbians in that vampire flick *The Hunger*, can only be a good thing.

Lesbians and the French.

Who knew? All I had to do was read the news, and already I'm getting tickled.

THE TROUBLE WITH TELETUBBIES

First it was those persistent rumors that Bert and Ernie, of Sesame Street fame, were a committed gay couple. Then Barney the Dinosaur was accused of leaning to the queer side for constantly repeating, "I love you very much!" And then it's Tinky Winky the Teletubby, outed by no less than the Reverend Jerry Falwell of Moral Majority fame.

According to reports, Falwell thinks that Tinky Winky, a member of PBS' Teletubby troupe, is a bad influence on the two-year-olds who watch the show. Falwell's evidence? Tinky Winky wears all purple (a gay color if ever there was one, Falwell says, though I think he'd have a heart attack if he saw our rainbow flag), has an antenna on his head in the shape of a triangle (another gay symbol in Falwell's lexicon, though personally I thought they had to be pink), and speaks with a boy's voice but carries a purse (though Falwell doesn't say it, apparently this means he thinks all gay men carry purses, a concept that is completely beyond me—and, boy, is he in for a surprise if he ever attends a gay rodeo, where not even the *women* carry purses!).

Never mind that the whispering about Bert and Ernie was long ago quashed by their puppeteer, Steven Whitmire, who was quoted years ago as saying, "They're puppets. They don't exist below the waist." (As if being gay is just a case of penis envy. Impotent gay puppets can still be in love. But I digress.) Barney's creators have issued similar denials.

The creators of the Teletubbies, PBS' shot at finally seeing some big merchandising bucks from a children's series, have been equally quick to respond that Falwell's charge is "absurd and kind of offensive." They say that Tinky Winky carries a "magic bag," not a purse. Though I have a priceless mental image of Bert and Ernie sharing a glass of Chardonnay with their beer-guzzling pals Barney and Tinky Winky—in a gay bar— when Bert says, "They found out about us years ago. Looks like they'll be on to our favorite purple couple soon. Barney and Tinky, you'll be the next Ellen and Anne!"

Interestingly, Falwell's gaydar is a bit late in coming. In Britain, the Teletubbies' original home, the mainstream newspapers were commenting in July of 1997 about Tinky Winky. *The Guardian* called Tinky Winky a "gay icon [who] prances around in a particularly camp fashion." The actor inside Tinky Winky was quickly replaced. Still, one Andy Medhurst, a lecturer at Sussex University, described Tinky Winky as "the first queer role model for toddlers."

The gay papers and magazines in the U.S. picked up on the story in 1998, with the *Advocate* writing in June that PBS was "clearly terrified that the same fundamentalists who boycott Disney are going to flip" when they hear about Tinky Winky. Never mind that the Disney boycott was a big old Goofy bust. And now Falwell has issued his warning. A gay Tinky Winky could somehow make our toddlers gay!

Now, while I disagree with Falwell that Tinky Winky's gay, and think that even if he were it shouldn't make a bit of difference, I have to think twice now about buying my three year old nephew the Teletubbies videos (which he loves) and the new interactive speak-and-sing-Teletubbies dolls-slash-action-figures (which he's definitely gonna want).

After all, I don't know if I want my nephew learning about gay folks from an individual (I can't safely say if Tinky Winky's a guy or a girl) attired in solid purple felt, carrying a lovely matching bag, and equipped with his own electronic toys in his belly. That's a bit too much for me. I wouldn't necessarily want him seeing drag queens—another part of the rich and varied gay culture—as an introduction to gay folks at large, either. At least, not unless they were of the *Too Wong Foo* or *The Birdcage* let's-rescue-the-young-folks-from-bad-hair-and-evil-papparazzi variety. (Which, admittedly, most drag queens I've met actually are.)

No, I'd prefer to leave his information about gay folks to his parents and me. Besides, Tinky Winky may only be a *practicing* homosexual, and I have no confidence in amateurs.

The interesting thing, though, about my nephew's fascination with the Teletubbies is that he seems to like all four of the Teletubbies equally well. It doesn't seem to matter at all that Tinky Winky carries a magic bag. My nephew doesn't react any differently to me, his gay uncle, either. To my way of thinking, that's pretty much as it should be.

Perhaps Jerry Falwell could learn a thing or two from a toddler and a Teletubby.

MY FAVORITE WHACKOS

"Ex-gay" is a lot like the concept of "former model." As a former model, you may not be working anymore, but you still know how to work it. Like it or not, some things just don't change.

Not everyone agrees. And if they don't get their way, sometimes they raise a ruckus. When the American Psychiatric Association recently cancelled a panel discussion on whether homosexuality can be "cured" through therapy, some self-described "former gays" got their panties in quite the wad. True, the American Psychiatric Association couldn't find any doctors who would argue for the "reorientation treatment," but that didn't stop the protest from Exodus International.

Exodus, you see, is an allegedly international group that seeks to help gay folks change their sexual orientation. Yup, they think that it's a matter of making a switch. Like from salsa to ketchup, perhaps.

Exodus' national board chairman, John Paulk, of Colorado Springs, Colorado, was outraged, according to the Associated Press. "I'm here as a representative of a virtually unseen but sizeable population," said Paulk. (Note to self: Is there maybe a reason that they're "unseen"? Is it the same reason as Santa Claus and the Tooth Fairy?) Paulk continued, "I once lived as a gay man, but now I'm [a re-oriented] heterosexual, something the American Psychological Association says does not exist."

The chairman described himself as a former drag queen who has two sons with his wife, a former lesbian. (Note to Paulk: As with former models, with drag queens, you can take the man out of the mascara, but you can't take the mascara out of the man. Maybe there's a reason you ended up with a former lesbian. Check to see who wears the pants.) Never mind the fact that several members of the Exodus and similar programs have left the group in highly publicized departures—after they fell in love with each other.

Paulk's group uses a religious conversion approach to "leaving the lifestyle." (Note to self: Need to spend some quality time determining what my "lifestyle" is, since I have absolutely no idea what that means.) But not all the groups out there take a Bible-beating approach. Just look at the International Healing Foundation, founded by a fellow named Richard Cohen, who was in a relationship with a man in the 1980's but then chose to live as a heterosexual. IHF suggests that no one is born gay, and that no one chooses to be gay, but that anyone can choose to be straight. Come again? Yes, IHF says that parents and environment are the causes of homosexuality. Now where have I heard this before? Hmmm. Could it be a tired, old rationale with a little re-packaging?

Besides, unhappy people who can come up with a reason for their unhappiness—like, that it was their gayness that made them unhappy—have an awful lot invested in proving that they made the right decision. They need to show the world that they didn't fail as a gay person—they just never should have been one. So they target the rest of us.

But these folks are not the only potholes on the road to the 21st century. Let's recall a little history. In 1935, Dr. Louis Max reported success with reparative therapy for homosexuals by using electroshock therapy at "intensities considerably higher than those usually employed on human subjects." (Bzzzzz!!) In 1966, counter-culture icon Timothy Leery suggested that LSD could be used to "repair" homosexuals." (Not so groovy, man.) Finally, in 1974, the American Psychiatric Association rather belatedly removed homosexuality from its list of disorders. (Analyze this!)

As I ponder the stunning absurdity of the "ex-gays," I have to take a page from their books and wonder, "What makes these people act this way?"

Maybe they just want to escape the status euphemistically referred to as "dating," which we all know can resemble hell on earth at times. Maybe they don't have the inner strength to face the challenges—being different, encountering discrimination, sometimes dealing with outright violence—that being gay calls upon us outwardly to face. Gay folks, you see, are necessarily courageous. Maybe some people don't have what it takes, so they duck, run, and throw stones at the rest of us.

Maybe they're like those poor, overweight women who are unhappy with their lives and run to the weight loss programs, which are often marketed as a way to fix their unhappiness. Sort of, "if I look like her, I'll have a happy life like that!" You just fixate on one aspect of yourself to convince yourself that THIS is why you're unhappy.

Maybe they really believe that the Christian Savior—who said not a single, solitary word about homosexuality in his 33 years on the planet—wants them to go out and make every other gay or lesbian person as miserably pathetic as they are themselves. Misery loves company, after all. Or perhaps it's even simpler than that.

Maybe they're just wackos.

Don't Ask, Don't Tell, Oh Brother!

I've always had a profound respect for the Armed Services.

A friend of mine in D.C. carries it even further. He took up jogging just so he could run along the river at the same time as an Army platoon (something about their butts looking like squirrels fighting under a blanket.)

Heck, I've even co-opted their slogans on many occasions: "Homosexuality. It's not just an Orientation—it's an Adventure!" And who could forget, "Be all that you can be—just go out with ME!"

But seriously, one of the most talked about issues of the last decade has been gays in the military. President George W. "Whiz Kid" Bush is openly opposed to changing "Don't Ask, Don't Tell," despite the fact that the ill-conceived scheme has been a dismal failure. Time was when Barry Goldwater, the grand dame of the Republican Party if ever there was one, declared that, "You don't have to be 'straight' to fight and die for your country. You just have to shoot straight." Well, I knew Barry Goldwater, Barry Goldwater was a friend of mine, and President Bush is no Barry Goldwater. (Okay, so I didn't know Goldwater, but that Lloyd Bentsen line from the '88 presidential campaign really seemed to fit.)

On the other side of the fence, in the last Presidential primary race, Senator Bill Bradley and Vice President Al Gore engaged in a grudge match to see who could score the most points with queer voters on the gays-in-the-military issue. Oddly—and refreshingly—Bradley and Gore were closer to the Goldwater view than Bush

Yet when it comes to gays in the military, I've always wondered what the big deal was anyway. Haven't any of the anti-gay-in-the-military folks ever read about ancient Greece—and the Army of Lovers from Thebes? The Army of Lovers was composed of male couples, who fought all the more ferociously to protect their partners. They were world renowned for their courage and valor. And for my money, a modern battalion of lesbians would be a phenomenal breakthrough. We could just threaten to send in the troops—when they're in the middle of synchronized PMS—and that should be enough to scare any biological warfare ideas right out of Saddam Hussein's head.

I happen to be a military brat myself, the son of a decorated war veteran. (Before I was old enough to understand about the medals thing, I thought that this meant the Army had assigned him an interior designer). For the first half of my childhood, Dad was still pursuing his military career. During most of those years, he had a commuter lifestyle, since the family was in a city and Dad was on a military base. My parents did the long-distance thing to give their kids some geographic stability, after they themselves had moved 28 times in the prior ten years. Serving your country is not an easy life.

Sometimes I would go to visit Dad on base. During one visit, he asked an enlisted man to keep up with me (one of the perks of command at the time, I suppose), and I promptly developed my first crush—or at least a six year old version thereof. Here was a big, strapping, good-looking guy who was kind to a child and could probably have protected me from a horde of invading Soviets. Little did I know that if I wanted to be like him or my Dad—the command thing had a certain appeal—when I grew up, my country wouldn't let me, just because I'm gay.

Although I don't see myself having a hankering to put on military fatigues any time soon, I think we gay folks should have the same right as the heterosexuals to kick the tar out of anybody who threatens our country.

After all, we can shoot straight, too.

Hoedown.
A Gathering of Friends, Family, and Some Crazy Folks You Don't Even Know

LIKE CAMP FOR QUEERS

In my continuing quest to learn about every option there is for gay travel, I recently went to camp. Queer camp, that is. And I have to tell you, queer camp looks an awful lot like Club Med.

My usual idea of a vacation is to plan a trip to one or two European cities where we go-go-go, see-see-see, do-do-do for a week or so. But after driving to three chateaux in France—in one day—last March, I needed a vacation from vacation. So I booked a trip through one of the gay vacation companies, RSVP. They were taking over Club Med at Playa Blanco on the western coast of Mexico for a week. I wouldn't have to think about where to go for meals, what to do for evening entertainment—or how to get a taxi back afterward. And there were lots of optional activities to keep me from boredom, like snorkeling, kayaking, sailing, and so forth. After all, I am not a beach person. (And as a pale-skinned blond, my Indian name is "Glows in the Dark.")

I went to Club RSVP with a buddy of mine, Robert. We discovered that Club RSVP did indeed have some elements of a camp experience. Such as the distinct lack of a hair dryer in the room. (What's a gay man to do? Aside from spending half an hour each morning in front of the air conditioning vent.) And sand crabs in the shower, which I escorted out of the room, their little feet clicking across the tile. Then there was the big, furry, fleshy spider that stared back at me from the sink one night as I was brushing my teeth. I let out a howl, and Robert woke up only long enough to say, "Just smack it." As Robert always says, "It's the top's job to catch the bugs." What were we to do? Sometimes you just gotta be versatile, so I trapped the big spider under a drinking glass for Robert's enjoyment the next morning. His reaction alone was worth the price of the trip.

But unlike the camp I remember as a child, this camp had about 450 gay men and 50 or so lesbians about. Ages ranged from 20's on up, and everyone was pleasant. You had to leave any attitude at the entrance to the open-air dining area, where you were seated randomly with new people. There was constantly something going on, and you could participate or not. (I spent a surprising amount of time under an umbrella on the beach, revising the proofs of *Tongue in Cheek and Other Places*. Hey, I am a beach person, after all.)

I tried new things, like snorkeling. I saw pretty fish, and managed not to get thrown against the rocks by the waves. I also swallowed so much salt water that I remembered why I don't like the taste of…well, you know. Robert and I kayaked and sailed and even rode horses (until we saw our spider's big brothers dangling from the tree branches).

There seemed be several basic types of guests at Club RSVP. There were the Honeymooners, who, as you might guess, were couples. Most days, the Honeymooners wore matching t-shirts. They were definitely the kind of folks who COULD admit to being co-dependent, but they'd have to check with each other first.

Then there were the Movers. These were invariably single—in fact, chronically so. I know of one Mover who went through five guys over the course of five days. Which, admittedly, wasn't as much of a challenge as it might seem, since he preferred to swim at the *shallow* end of the pool.

And of course, there were the Shakers. I paid the Club Med photographer five bucks for a photo of a tall, dark, handsome and muscled Texan I never even met. In the costume contest, he came as excess baggage—wearing only a strategically placed fanny pack. Need I say more?

One of the nicest things about the evenings was the nightly entertainment. It was actually good. Hosted by a San Francisco comedian named Danny Williams, whose humor kept me rolling, there were singers and comedians and a funny drag performer. Then there was nightly disco, if you were so inclined.

Perhaps the best aspect of the trip was meeting people I really enjoyed hanging out with and being surrounded by a ton of other gay folks in a community-styled atmosphere. Sure, a trip like that can be about seeing new places (and doing new people there, for the Movers and Shakers, especially).

But it's also about something else we don't find too often in the midst of a straight world—a sense of togetherness and fun, in a lovely and safe place. Like camp for queers.

OUT AT WORK?

Are you an in-ee or an out-ee? No, I'm not asking about your navel. This is a "family" column, and that would be T.M.I. (too much information). I mean, are you out at work?

I'm not asking whether you hang gay flags from your cubicle wall or whether you've stenciled pink triangles along the moldings in your office. Instead, at the office are you as comfortable about being a queer person as your hetero colleagues are about being straight?

Because surprisingly many writers are not Stephen King or fully-employed journalists, we generally have day jobs. I pay my rent by working as a lawyer (albeit, as one of the cooler, hipper lawyers out there—not like there's much competition). A couple of years ago, after a few years of contract work, I found what appeared to be a really interesting corporate job opening. Since I've never exactly been "in," I decided to be "out" from the git-go. When I submitted legal writing samples along with my resume, I included a case analysis I wrote for *Lesbian/Gay Law Notes*. I figured that would give my prospective employers at least a hint, and if I wasn't wanted because I'm gay, then I'd know pretty quick and wouldn't waste anybody's time, least of all my own.

Turned out it wasn't an issue, and the job and the would-be colleagues were great. But when I got the offer, there was one thing still to do. Great job or no, I needed more evidence. I picked up the phone and called Human Resources.

"Hello," I said. "I'd like to get a copy of your non-discrimination statement."

"Is there anything particular you're looking for? Maybe I can tell you now before I send it," the annoyingly helpful person replied.

"Um, yes, actually. I want to know if sexual orientation is included."

"Oh," she replied cheerily, "why, yes, I believe it is."

Right, honey, I thought, It's not in most companies' statements. You probably never get the question and are like the girl in law school who asked me, "Is sexual orientation discrimination like gender discrimination?" But I thanked her and asked her to fax me the statement, and sure enough, sexual orientation was included. I immediately called and accepted the job.

And incidentally, the first time I saw the HR person in the hallway at work, she stopped and said, "You found the term you were looking for in our statement, didn't you?" She smiled the biggest "I told you so" smile I'd ever seen.

I grinned and nodded that I had. "You were right," I said.

"Thought so," she replied perkily, and trotted off.

I've never regretted taking the job. In fact, I've really enjoyed it. I work for the best boss in the world. (And I plan to show her this column.) Seriously, my boss is a Harvard-educated lawyer and a card-carrying ACLU member. She's as much a mentor as a manager, and I'm constantly learning from her. Equally important, since I have no need to pretend to be straight, I'm actually able to focus all my energy on learning and (hopefully) excelling at my job.

That's the key aspect of being open about—and protected against discrimination for—your sexual orientation at work. In essence, my status as a gay person makes no more difference than any of my co-workers' status(es) as straight, female, Jewish, Christian or African-American. I do a great job at my company, I learn from my colleagues, and I'm not distracted by something as absurd as "Will I lose my job because I'm gay?"

To paraphrase Bill Clinton's old campaign slogan, "It's the productivity, stupid." Which, aside from being good for me, is great for the company. I work for a manager who recognizes that fact, and in a company where non-discrimination is the written policy.

Someday, of course, all companies will be that way. Notice I say "will be" rather than "might be." As long as the job market continues to remain tight, and as long as queer kids entering the work force keep becoming less and less tolerant of being closeted of discrimination, companies will have to be that way to keep the best employees, some of whom are—surprise—queer. The policy at my company gives me greater incentive to stay there. I would never move to a company without it. (Just don't tell my boss that before my next review. Talk about undercutting your negotiational strength.)

So tell me, now. Lean in close, if you want. Are you an in-ee or an out-ee?

SENSE AND SENSIBILITY

My best friend is on safari in Africa. A photo safari, since she's a fairly devout animal rights kind of woman.

When she told me she was planning to go on a safari, my better gay self had visions of charming bungalows in well-stocked compounds, strategically placed throughout the wild open plains. From which, every morning, you would leave in your Range Rover with your trusty—and well-armed—guide named Rick (they're always named Rick, aren't they?), returning safely to the comforts of the compound each night after a long day of exploration and adventure.

But my illusions were quickly shattered when she informed me, in her most matter of fact voice, that this wasn't that sort of safari. No, it's a put up your tent in the rain kind of safari. The bring your own bio-degradable toilet paper but we don't have outhouses kind of safari. I was aghast.

Now, I should explain that my friend has always been a hotel and blow dryer kind of gal. A girl whom I used to accompany to Tiffany's in New York City every now and then, so that we could try on wedding rings in anticipation of the day that one or both of us gets to walk down that aisle. That was our idea of being prepared, in the best of boy scout traditions. You get the idea.

Yet, at this very moment, that same girl is sleeping on the ground in a tent in the wilds of Africa. She has not had a shower in over a week. And it's her time of the month.

No, I'm not worried about her surviving Africa. I'm a lot more worried about Africa surviving her.

But it does illustrate a point. What point, you might ask? It's quite obvious, I answer. That generally speaking, gay men have more sense than straight women. And we should know, since a lot of us have them as best or at least very good friends. (Besides, I can say that since mine's in Africa.)

Seriously, though, the chances are virtually nil that knowing myself as I do, you would ever catch me on a three week, no facilities, how bad can you smell kind of holiday. I would have sense enough to leave that to my butchier gay brethren, who might actually enjoy wearing the same pair of underwear for a week at a time. As for me, when it comes to camping, I've never understood where you're supposed to plug in the electric razor.

Need I say more?

Okay, I see you're not convinced. So answer me this: what gay man in his right mind would have played hide the cigar outside the Oval Office with Bill Clinton? *Bill Clinton!* Eeeee—eeeuw!

Need more convincing? What gay man would ever have considered marrying the likes of Pat Robertson? Newt Gingrich? Rush Limbaugh? *Dennis Rodman?* Yet some poor besotted straight woman did.

And who, I might ask, is responsible for the incomprehensible popularity and success of Michael Flatley, Lord of the Dance? (Double eeeee—eeeuw!) Who is responsible for making Leonardo di Caprio, a pretty but barely post-pubescent child, into an international sex symbol after *Titanic?* The answer is straight women, of course.

To be fair, it is true that there are an awful lot of gay men with straight female best friends out there, and vice versa. Sort of a legion of Will and Grace's, though without the prime-time time slot or the super-queer friend named Jack. (A TV show which, I admit, I watch religiously.) And that fact alone should speak volumes about the sensibility of those same straight women.

So I guess I should keep my point to myself when my best friend returns from her African safari. Besides, she'll probably tell me all about some fascinating experience she had in the wild—like getting caught in a stampede of zebras, or having a fireside fling with the guide, named Rick.

And I'll think, "Hmm. Maybe I should consider a safari of the same sort, after all. Where we camp. And don't bathe. For days and days and days and days."

Then my gay sense will intervene and stop my in my tracks. Besides, the African continent could never survive both of us.

OH, MOTHER!

I decided to take my mother to New York City for her birthday. I was worried. Not about Mom surviving the City. I was worried about the City surviving my mother.

My mom and I have always had a close relationship. We live in different cities, but we usually manage to talk at least once a week. (I'd call my dad more often too, but that hearing loss of his means the neighbors hear all my conversation, as I yell into the phone. I'm usually hoarse by the end.) As I've gotten older—and so has she—we've evolved into something akin to a parent-child friendship. (I forgave her years ago for those disco-dancing lessons with her when I was 12.)

Mother has always been a person who speaks her mind, and I appreciate that. I think I inherited something of it as well. (Ask any of my ex-boyfriends.) Sometimes it's a mixed blessing. Like the time we were having a clinical discussion of men's penises. (I forget how it came up.) She mentioned something specific about the size of Dad's. My eyes widened, and I thought to myself, "Well, *that's* another couple years of therapy for me." But at least I'm pretty sure she's always been honest with me.

There's been only one time in my life when I was surprised by an unexpected reaction from Mom. When I first came out to her at age twenty, my mother, an avowed intellectual, suddenly morphed into a fundamentalist preacher. She blamed my gayness on France, where I'd just spent a year in school and confirmed—ooh, la, la!—that I was definitely "*un homosexuel.*" (Mom's never looked at French food the same since.) But after a couple years of drama, and the realization that it really wasn't a phase or some unanticipated side effect of eating escargot, she came around.

I never had to worry about being cut off—which would not have been fun during college—and there was never any question that I was loved no matter what. I got none of the major ugliness that I've heard about other kids getting from their parents. Mine believed that you love your children. Period. (In fact, the person who had the most fun during those two years was my sister, who was supportive but quite obviously pleased that the "perfect" older brother she'd been tolerating all these years had finally done something the parents were upset about. Hey, I was just doing my part to help out.)

These days, Mom's not marching in Pride Parades, but she does do her part. She and Dad stopped eating at Cracker Barrel when the discrimination against gays and lesbians came out. More recently, Mom wrote a letter to the editor of the city newspaper in response to an anti-gay viewpoint article. She was harshly critical of the article and supportive of her gay son. It got published. Under her name. In Memphis, Tennessee. And she's Baptist. I'd say that took balls.

So for her birthday, we went to New York City, for a long weekend of sightseeing, museums, a Broadway show, and a Greenwich Village comedy club. Mom is one of those people who gets so into seeing things that she's up at the crack of dawn and ready to go. ("You're sleepy? Well, so was I. But once you get up and shower, you'll wake right up!") And I usually forget to bring my tranquilizer darts.

In a five day stretch, we saw every museum known to man. The Museum of Modern Metropolitan Guggenheim Fricke Art, I think. (It all runs together.) We shopped up and down Fifth Avenue. We took photos of Rockefeller Center from the sixth floor window of Saks 5th Avenue. We went to the top of the Empire State Building and the World Trade Center. We saw *Chicago* on Broadway, where we sat beside a nice gay couple and Mom proved once again she has no gaydar. ("You think they were gay? I thought he was just helping his friend out of the chair." Plausible, I guess, since one had crutches, but…)

We lunched in the Village, near Stonewall, which I pointed out. ("Oh, look at those two pretty men holding hands, Kevin." "Those are lesbians, Mom. With shaved heads and tattoos.") At the comedy club, we saw comedians from *Saturday Night Live*—who were actually funny doing stand-up. Whenever they ventured into the topic of gay folks, Mom would glance at me and look ready to pounce, in case it should prove to be an anti-gay joke. (Fortunately, there weren't any.)

After five days in New York, Mom was reluctantly ready to hit the road. When she got home, she was so exhausted that she didn't get out of bed until eight o'clock the following evening. But that evening, she called me. There was one question on her mind. "So where are we going next year?"

Oh, Mother!

THE GAYING OF GOD

Time was when gays and God went together like genius and President George W. Bush—in other words, not at all.

But ole Dubya has been looking pretty bright lately in his political successes in Washington. When Senator Ted Kennedy speaks glowingly about a Bush education plan, you have to wonder if G.W.'s not so dumb after all. (My personal jury is still out on that question, I must admit, but I'm "hopefuller" that he's just really bad with grammar.)

Not unlike Georgie Boy's close brush with intelligence, gays and religion keep on flirting and, in some instances, openly flaunting their relationship. This is, as you might expect, much to the dismay of some straight folks, who would prefer that the relationship be kept a little more discreet, and a little less in-your-face. A little more closeted. More like a Republican politician's clandestine extra-marital affair. (Sorry, Newt—but for the record, as a humorist, I really miss ya.)

I remember that not so very long ago, the words "gay and lesbian" weren't very far removed from "fire and brimstone," or "hell and damnation," or my personal favorite, "abomination in the sight of God." Of course, I always thought that being an abomination was a good thing. After all, I loved the Abominable Snowman in *Rudolph, the Red-Nosed Reindeer.*

But these days, choice is the word. There are gay Jewish synagogues, specifically gay Christian churches like the Metropolitan Community Church, gay Buddhists, gay Wiccans, and gay affirming local Christian churches from Unitarian to Methodist. (If I've left anyone out, I'm blond, and I just can't keep up.)

133

For years, though, the Southern Baptists have been on the shallow end of the intelligence pool when it comes to homosexuality. Hey, a church opposed to dancing isn't likely to appreciate the folks who gave the world The Village People. But in Atlanta, the heart of the New South, something a little queer has happened to the Southern Baptists.

You see, two Southern Baptist churches in Atlanta at Oakhurst and Virginia-Highland were recently charged by the Atlanta Baptist Association with "affirming and approving and endorsing homosexual behavior." (Sends shivers down your spine, doesn't it? Sort of hearkens back to the Spanish Inquisition, minus the iron shackles and the burning at the stake. At least, I THINK it's minus the shackles and the burning at the stake.) In the category of what-you-get-from-affirming, I should note that when Virginia-Highland began its outreach to the gay community, it was a dying church. Now the choir is filled with basses, tenors, and baritones who come to practice regularly. The minister's delighted.

After the charge was made, however, the truly surprising thing is what happened next. The Atlanta Baptist Association voted NOT to expel the two offending churches. And it wasn't even a close vote. Hallelujah!

"I think this is a reminder to the world that Baptists are a diverse people," said the Reverend Tim Shirley of Virginia-Highland, who celebrated the victory with the minister from Oakhurst with back-slapping and a hug in the parking lot. (A nicely queer touch, I thought.) "Homosexuality," said Rev. Shirley, "is a completely natural orientation and not a chosen behavior or lifestyle," and the association doesn't have to agree in order to retain the two churches. (Yes, that statement came from the mouth of a Southern Baptist minister.)

Of course, now the Georgia and the Southern Baptist associations may vote to expel the Atlanta association from their fold—to avoid being gay by association, I suppose, if you'll pardon the pun. (Their motto: "Our butts are sore from wooden pews—and NOTHING ELSE, thank you very much.") As if that weren't enough, several of the Atlanta churches who voted for expulsion may also take their holy marbles and go home to form their own presumably anti-gay association in protest.

But "blessing does not require agreement," said a tired Rev. Shirley. "It does require understanding." So maybe the gaying of God is leading to more understanding and inclusion for gays and lesbians. Maybe it's leading to more ways for gay folks who believe to share their faith with others, whether those others are gay or straight.

And that may be the best blessing of all.

WISH LISTS

Every year, my best friend and I each write down a wish list of what we want to accomplish during the next year. Then we mail the list to each other. So that the following year we can go through the lists (with no cheating) to see how close—or not—we each came to getting the things we wished for.

Now she's a little on the conservative side in her wishes. Personally, I think she just likes to say, "See, I got more than you did." Which is why I always like to add things in to her list after I receive it. Items like, "Meet the man of my day dreams. Show him the wonderful creature I am and awaken his uncontrollable desire to have me in his life until death do us part, or incapacitate him with tranquilizer darts, as needed. Get married in a Vera Wang dress in a big church wedding that will make the Charles and Diana nuptials look like a Las Vegas quickie." She typically rolls her eyes and ignores my additions, when the time for the annual Reading of the Lists arrives.

But I never limit myself in my wish lists, because if you limit your dreams, you limit your realities. (Hey, some people pay big bucks to motivational speakers for that little statement of the obvious.) I cover as broad a range as possible, from the concrete to the abstract, so that I know I'll get at least a few. Then I ad-lib a little.

My wish list this year went something like this: Travel to interesting places in far away lands, preferably of the European persuasion. Do lots of interesting things and people there. (Sorry, that should have been "meet people there.")

Shop for a condo or townhouse, thereby totally freaking boyfriend out. Spend more quality time with (not to mention on and in) boyfriend. Be happy with my boyfriend and accept his frailties—God knows he has to deal with mine. Do our damnedest to work things out in our relationship, because we love each other so much.

Visit family more often, after doubling frequency of sessions with qualified therapist. See nephew more frequently and contribute monthly amounts to his stock fund.

Personally determine whether San Francisco is the Sodom that the Christian Right claims it is. Send postcards to all my friends.

Laugh a lot (with people, not at them). Cry as little as possible.

Sell a few copies of *It Only Hurts When I Polka: Even More Humorous Looks at Queer Life.* Prepare Lambda Literary Award acceptance speech for same. (Just in case. As I said, you gotta throw in a few big ones to make it interesting.) Finish novel. Accept Pulitzer.

Adapt *It Only Hurts When I Polka* into widely acclaimed off-Broadway show, finally proving that sketches of gay life can be funny, entertaining, and moving without involving AIDS or coming out.

Which I figure covers pretty much all the bases. But just as I have a personal wish list, I also have a similar gay and lesbian wish list, that I update every year, especially around Pride Month.

At the top of my queer wish list is passage of ENDA, the Employment Nondiscrimination Act. Fear of being fired because you're gay or lesbian is not a happy thing. If we can get rid of that fear, a lot more people will waltz out of the closet. Thus increasing dating possibilities for us all. (Hey, you have to have priorities.)

Not far behind ENDA is legalized marriage for gays and lesbians. We've already got civil unions in Vermont, and if we don't dream it, we'll never get it. Besides, I know a lot of gold-digging husband hunters out there breathlessly awaiting those support and inheritance rights that come with marriage. (Granted, these are people whose idea of foreplay is uttering lines like, "Honey, how is that oxygen tent doing for you?" And, "Can I get you some more prunes?")

I'm also wishing that George W. Bush turns over a new leaf and embraces gay equality as a meaningful objective for an American president. (Again, you gotta think big.)

I'm hoping for even more exposure on TV and in movies and in the popular culture, so that no young gay or lesbian person will ever have to question themselves or their right to a happy life. Because they'll see that Will, and not just Grace, CAN date another man.

Finally, I'm hoping that no more of our fellow gay and lesbian folks will have to fall at the hands of a still-deadly disease.

I'm pretty proud of my wish lists. And I can't wait to find out how many come true.

ABOUT THE AUTHOR

Kevin Isom is the author of *Tongue in Cheek and Other Places: A Seriously Humorous Look at Queer Life.* He writes a syndicated humor column, "Tongue in Cheek," which appears in newspapers and magazines across the United States, Australia, and Canada. His essays, fiction and articles have appeared in numerous reviews and anthologies, including the *Harvard Gay & Lesbian Review* and others. He recently finished a novel, "Like Fruit on the Vine." He may be reached at via email at *Isomonline@aol.com* or on the web at http://kevinisom.freeyellow.com.